HEALTHY VEGAN PERSIAN RECIPE

COPYRIGHT ©2014 BY BRYAN RYLEE.
ALL RIGHTS RESERVED. NO PART OF THIS BOOK MAY BE USED OR REPRODUCED IN ANY MATTER WHATSOEVER WITHOUT PERMISSION IN WRITING FROM THE AUTHOR EXCEPT IN THE CASE OF BRIEF QUOTATIONS
EMBODIED IN CRITICAL ARTICLES OR REVIEW.

DISCLAIMER:

THE INFORMATION PRESENTED IN THIS BOOK REPRESENTS THE VIEWS OF THE PUBLISHER AS OF THE DATE OF PUBLICATION. THE PUBLISHER RESERVES THE RIGHTS TO ALTER UPDATE THEIR OPINIONS BASED ON NEW CONDITIONS. THIS REPORT IS FOR INFORMATIONAL PURPOSES ONLY. THE AUTHOR AND THE PUBLISHER DO NOT ACCEPT ANY RESPONSIBILITIES FOR ANY LIABILITIES RESULTING FROM THE USE OF THIS INFORMATION. WHILE EVERY ATTEMPT HAS BEEN MADE TO VERIFY THE INFORMATION PROVIDED HERE, THE AUTHOR AND THE PUBLISHER CANNOT ASSUME ANY RESPONSIBILITY FOR ERRORS, INACCURACIES OR OMISSIONS. ANY SIMILARITIES WITH PEOPLE OR FACTS ARE UNINTENTIONAL.

TABLE OF CONTENTS

Introduction

The Persian Cuisine – Most Common Ingredients 10
Appetizers 13
Walnut and Cucumber Creamy Salad 13
Artichoke Heart Dip... 14
Baba Ganoush 16
Green Avocado Dip on Toasted Bread................................ 18
Beet and Walnut Dip.. 19
Red Bell Pepper Hummus... 20
Eggplant and Tomato Fry Up... 22
Potato Creamy Salad... 23
Tofu and Tomato Kebabs 25
Roasted Garlic Spread... 26
Salads 27
Orzo and Green Olive Salad 27
Fattoush Salad 28
Persian Carrot Salad.. 30
Sumac Tomato Salad 31
Persian Chickpea Salad... 32
Shirazi Salad 34
Fresh Farro Salad 35
Persian Rice and Cucumber Salad 36
Soups and Stews.. 37
Persian Herb Soup.. 37
Persian Mushroom Stew 38
Persian Barley Soup – Ash-e-jow 39
Pomegranate Soup.. 41
Cold Cucumber Soup 42
Persian Pistachio Soup 44
Persian Herbed Bean Soup.. 45
Tofu Spinach Soup 46
Bean and Mushroom Stew.. 48

Rhubarb Stew 49
Persian Eggplant Stew 50
Persian Celery and Potato Stew 52
Lentil and Beet Soup with Flour Dumplings 53
Eggplant and Green Grape Stew 54
Main Dishes 55
Veggie Stuffed Bell Peppers 55
Persian Potato Gratin 57
Potato and Prune Casserole 59
Kateh – Persian Rice 60
Pomegranate Roasted Tofu 61
Saffron Baked Mushrooms 62
Walnut and Rice Balls 63
Persian Pilaf 65
Vegetable Curry 67
Fried Eggplant Casserole 69
Falafel Loaf 70
Persian Okra Stew 72

Persian Veggie Cabbage Rolls 73
Couscous Stuffed Tomatoes 75
Basmati Rice with Potato Crust 77
Jeweled Rice 78
Stuffed Eggplants 79
Desserts 80
Persian Melon Popsicles 80
Spiced Rice Pudding 81
Persian Chickpea Flour Cookies 82
Persian Halva 84
Spiced Carrot Halva 86
Cinnamon Date Cake 88
Wild Rice Apricot Pudding 90
Melon and Cherry Compote 91
Persian Sweet Rice 92
Ranginak – Date and Walnut Squares 93

Conclusion 94

Introduction

THE PERSIAN CUISINE INCLUDES TWO MAIN GEOGRAPHIC AREAS: PERSIA AND IRAN, AND IT IS A CUISINE THAT HAS BEEN STRONGLY INFLUENCED BY SURROUNDING AREAS, INCLUDING THE TURKISH CUISINE OR THE MEDITERRANEAN ONE, BUT ALSO INDIAN AND ASIAN. SO MUCH THAT YOU WILL FIND COMMON INGREDIENTS IN ALL OF THEM AND SOMETIMES IT IS HARD TO SAY WHICH CUISINE HAS INFLUENCED THE OTHER. BUT A FACT REMAINS – THE OLD PERSIAN ARCHIVES NAME CORIANDER, SAFFRON, CUMIN, MINT, POMEGRANATES, PISTACHIO AND EVEN OLIVE OIL AS PRODUCTS THAT WERE TRADED IN THE OLD DAYS OF THE PERSIAN EMPIRE, THEREFORE WE CAN SAY THAT THE PERSIAN CUISINE IS ANCIENT AND VARIED.

AMONGST THE STAPLE INGREDIENTS OF THE PERSIAN CUISINE YOU WILL FIND: FRESH HERBS, PLUMS, POMEGRANATES, PRUNES, APRICOTS, RAISINS, RICE, VEGETABLES, NUTS, SAFFRON, CINNAMON AND PARSLEY. THEY ARE COMBINED IN UNUSUAL WAYS SOMETIMES BUT IN THE END EVERY PERSIAN DISH IS FLAVORFUL AND RICH, DELICIOUS AND SPECIAL AND ALL YOU HAVE TO DO IS TASTE AND BE HOOKED!

ONE OF THE MOST COMMON PERSIAN INGREDIENTS, FOUND IN MANY DISHES, BOTH MEAT AND VEGAN ONES IS RICE. RICE WAS FIRST BROUGHT TO THE REGION FROM INDIA BUT IT SOON GAINED TERRAIN WITH THE LOCALS. ALTHOUGH AT FIRST IT WAS MOSTLY USED BY THE UPPER CLASS OF THE SOCIETY, IN THE LAST DECADES IT BECAME MORE ACCESSIBLE,

EVEN TO THE POOR PEOPLE WHO WENT FROM CONSUMING MOSTLY BREAD TO EATING RICE AS A BASE FOOD.

THERE ARE VARIOUS WAYS OF COOKING RICE IN THE PERSIAN CUISINE. POLO DESIGNATES THE RICE THAT IS COOKED BY SOAKING IT IN SALTED WATER FOR A FEW HOURS. THE RICE IS THEN STEAMED TO PREPARE A FLUFFY RICE THAT IT'S NOT STICKY AT ALL. THIS TYPE OF COOKED RICE IS USUALLY SERVED SIMPLE OR AS A SIDE DISH. THE SECOND WAY OF COOKING RICE INVOLVES BOILING IT IN WATER UNTIL THE LIQUID IS COMPLETELY ABSORBED. THIS METHOD IS PROBABLY THE SIMPLEST OF ALL AND IT YIELDS A SIMPLE, BASIC RICE THAT WORKS GREAT WITH SAUCES OR MOIST, JUICY DISHES. THE LAST WAY OF COOKING RICE IS CALLED *DAMY* AND IT IS VERY SIMILAR TO *KATEH* WITH THE DIFFERENCE THAT FOR *DAMY* OTHER INGREDIENTS CAN BE ADDED – NUTS, DRIED FRUITS OR VEGETABLES ARE THE MOST BASIC ADDITIONAL INGREDIENTS. OFTEN, THE RICE IS COOKED UNTIL A HARD CRUST FORMS AT THE BOTTOM – *TAH DIG*.

APART FROM RICE, BREAD IS ALSO A BIG PART OF THE PERSIAN CUISINE. THE GENERIC TERM FOR BREAD IN PERSIAN IS *NAN* WHICH YOU ARE FAMILIAR WITH SINCE *NAAN* BREAD IS AVAILABLE WORLDWIDE NOWADAYS. PERSIAN BREAD IS USUALLY ROUND OR OVAL AND FLAT AND IT IS BAKED ON A SPECIAL GRILL STOVE OR STONE. SOMETIME IS SO THIN THAT IT GOES CRISPY. BUT NO MATTER THE TYPE, BREAD IS A HUGE PART OF A MEAL IN THE PERSIAN CUISINE AND THAT SHOULDN'T BE NEGLECTED.

SINCE IT HAS MEDITERRANEAN INFLUENCES TOO, THE PERSIAN CUISINE MAKES USE OF A LOT OF FRESH FRUITS AND VEGETABLES. TRADITIONALLY, PERSIANS WOULD SERVE A BOWL OF FRESH FRUITS AT EVERY

MEAL WHILE VEGGIES ARE THE MAIN SIDE DISHES SERVED TO MOST MEALS. BUT FROM ALL THE AVAILABLE VEGETABLES, THE EGGPLANT IS THE MOST COMMON ONE. IN FACT, IT IS SO USED IN THE PERSIAN CUISINE THAT SOME PEOPLE CALL IT "THE POTATO OF PERSIA". IT IS COOKED IN WAYS THAT YOU WOULDN'T EXPECT AND IT TASTES GREAT.

BUT A PERSIAN DISH WOULDN'T BE THE SAME WITHOUT THE AROMATIC FRESH HERBS. PARSLEY, CILANTRO AND MINT ARE THE THREE MAIN HERBS USED IN ANYTHING, FROM SOUPS TO DIPS, MAIN DISHES AND SALADS. THEY ADD FRESHNESS AND MAKE DISHES LIGHTER AND HIGHLY FRAGRANT. AND SINCE WE ARE TALKING ABOUT GIVING FLAVOR TO THE FOOD, WE CAN'T NEGLECT SPICES, CAN WE?! THEY ARE VERY IMPORTANT IN MOST ORIENTAL CUISINES AND THE PERSIAN ONE IS ONE OF THEM. CINNAMON, CUMIN, SAFFRON, HOT PEPPERS AND SUMAC ARE JUST A FEW OF THE MOST USED SPICES. THEIR MAIN GOAL IS TO ADD A FRAGRANT TOUCH TO ANY DISH BUT NEVER OVERPOWER IT. ON THEIR OWN SPICES TEND TO BE INTENSE AND BOLD, BUT IN PERSIAN DISHES THEY ARE DELICATE AND SUBTLE, SUPPORTING OTHER INGREDIENTS RATHER THAN THEM BECOMING THE STARS OF THE DISH.

AN INTERESTING FACT ABOUT THE PERSIAN CUISINE IS HOW PEOPLE USED TO CHOOSE THEIR DAILY FOOD COMBINATIONS. THEY BELIEVED THAT KEEPING A BALANCE BETWEEN HOT AND COLD OR DRY AND WET IN DIET IS THE KEY TO A HEALTHY BODY AND MIND, THEREFORE THEY ALWAYS TRIED TO COMBINE A HOT FOOD WITH A COLD ONE. FAT, MEAT, WHEAT, SUGAR, DRIED FRUITS AND VEGETABLES WERE CONSIDERED HOT FOODS WHILE BEEF, RICE, DAIRY PRODUCTS AND SOME FRESH FRUITS AND VEGGIES WERE CONSIDERED COLD FOODS. WHENEVER A MENU WAS PLANNED, THIS

PRINCIPLE WAS TAKEN INTO CONSIDERATION SO THEY ALWAYS ENDED UP WITH ONE HOT FOOD AND ONE COLD FOOD ON THEIR PLATE.

AS FOR VEGANS WANTING TO EAT PERSIAN FOODS, WORRY NOT CAUSE THERE ARE PLENTY OF VEGAN RECIPES FOR EVERY TASTE OUT THERE. FROM SIMPLE RICE DISHES TO VEGETABLE DISHES, YOU WILL FIND SOMETHING TO FIT YOUR TASTE AND NEEDS IN THIS WIDE RANGE OF DISHES, ALL WITH AN AMAZING FLAVOR AND TEXTURE, ALL COLORFUL AND NUTRITIOUS.

BOTTOM LINE IS THAT THE PERSIAN CUISINE IS EXOTIC AND COLORFUL, VARIED AND FRAGRANT, FLAVORFUL AND BALANCED, IT IS A CUISINE THAT WILL TEACH ALL ABOUT SPICES, HERBS AND FRESH INGREDIENTS, A CUISINE THAT SOMEHOW MANAGES TO BALANCE INGREDIENTS THAT YOU RARELY THINK OF. ALL YOU HAVE TO DO IS KEEP AN OPEN MIND AND A BOLD PALATE AND TRY THE RECIPES FOUND IN THIS BOOK. THEY'VE ALL BEEN DESIGNED TO ACCOMMODATE THE NEEDS OF A VEGAN IN SEARCH FOR PERSIAN RECIPES SO GO AHEAD AND START COOKING. I'M SURE YOU WILL FIND A FAVORITE AMONGST THESE RECIPES!

The Persian Cuisine – Most Common Ingredients

GREEN HERBS – PARSLEY, CORIANDER, CILANTRO AND MINT ARE THE MAIN GREEN HERBS USED IN THE PERSIAN CUISINE. THEY ARE EASY TO FIND ALL YEAR AROUND IN MOST MARKETS OR SUPERMARKETS, BUT YOU CAN ALSO GROW THEM AT HOME IF YOU WANT. APART FROM THEIR INTENSE AND FRESH TASTE, GREEN HERBS ARE ALSO GREAT SOURCES OF ANTIOXIDANTS AND VITAMINS WHICH IS A GREAT ADVANTAGE IN SALADS FOR INSTANCE.

RICE – THERE ARE MANY VARIETIES OF RICE OUT THERE, BUT THE PERSIAN CUISINE USES BASMATI RICE MOSTLY. IT'S EASY TO COOK AND HAS A DELICATE TASTE THAT GOES WITH MOST FOODS. IF YOU'RE LOOKING FOR A HEALTHIER OPTION THOUGH, YOU CAN GO FOR WILD RICE WHICH HAS A MORE FLAVORFUL AROMA AS WELL.

SAFFRON – SAFFRON IS AN EXPENSIVE SPICE BECAUSE IT COMES FROM A RARE CROCUS. ONLY THE STEMS OF THE CROCUS ARE USED AND FOR THAT REASON CULTIVATING IT IS DIFFICULT. ITS TASTE IS OFTEN DESCRIBED AS HONEY WITH GRASSY NOTES. APART FROM TASTE, SAFFRON ALSO ADDS A BEAUTIFUL YELLOW-ORANGE COLOR TO ANY FOOD IS BEING USED INTO. BE CAREFUL WHEN BUYING IT THOUGH. SAFFRON IS USUALLY PACKED IN FOIL TO PROTECT FROM AIR AND LIGHT AND ONCE BOUGHT IT SHOULD BE STORED IN AIRTIGHT CONTAINERS AND DARK PLACES.

TURMERIC – ALSO KNOWN AS *CURCUMA* OR *CURCUMIN*,

TURMERIC IS A BRIGHT YELLOW POWDER MADE FROM TURMERIC RHIZOMES. IT IS AN ANCIENT SPICE THAT HAS BEEN USED IN INDIA AND SURROUNDING COUNTRIES FOR CENTURIES. IT HAS NO CALORIES AND ZERO CHOLESTEROL BUT IT IS RICH IN FIBERS, IRON, MAGNESIUM AND VITAMIN B. TURMERIC IS A GREAT SUBSTITUTE FOR SAFFRON IN TERMS OF COLOR, BUT NOT TASTE.

SUMAC – SUMAC IS LEMONY AND SALTY, A GREAT PERSIAN SPICE USED IN MANY RECIPES, FROM SALADS TO STEWS. IT IS OFTEN USED TO GIVE A CERTAIN TARTNESS TO FOODS, ALONG WITH POMEGRANATE JUICE OR SYRUP.

DRIED FRUITS – USED IN BOTH SAVORY AND SWEET DISHES, DRIED FRUITS ARE A GREAT SOURCE OF NUTRIENTS, FROM FIBERS TO VITAMINS AND MINERALS, BUT THEY ALSO PACK A LOT OF FLAVOR, USUALLY MORE FLAVOR THAN THE ACTUAL FRESH FRUITS JUST BECAUSE THEY ARE PICKED WHEN IN SEASON THEN DRIED SO THE FLAVOR INTENSIFIES AND THE AROMA IS PRESERVED. PLUS, THEY ARE EASY TO STORE IN AN AIRTIGHT CONTAINER IN YOUR CUPBOARD AND USED IN SALADS OR EVEN STEWS.

NUTS – ALMONDS, PISTACHIO AND WALNUTS ARE THREE OF THE MOST USED NUTS IN THE PERSIAN CUISINE. EITHER USED IN COOKING OR AS A SNACK, THEY ARE A GREAT SOURCE OF FIBERS AND GOOD FATS AND HAVE A RICH AROMA THAT WORKS WITH MOST FOODS.

EGGPLANTS – AS MENTIONED ABOVE, THE EGGPLANTS ARE CONSIDERED "THE POTATOES OF PERSIAN", BUT THEY HAVE FAR MORE NUTRITIOUS THAN POTATOES. IRON, CALCIUM AND FIBERS ARE JUST A FEW OF THE NUTRIENTS FOUND IN EGGPLANTS. IT'S BEEN PROVED

THAT A REGULAR INTAKE OF EGGPLANTS BOOSTS YOUR DIGESTIVE SYSTEM, BUT FURTHERMORE, EGGPLANTS HAVE LITTLE CALORIES AND LESS CARBS THAN OTHER VEGGIES.

HOWEVER, THIS IS JUST A SHORT LIST. AS LONG AS YOU USE SPICES AND HERBS YOU CAN CALL ANY RECIPE PERSIAN BECAUSE THOSE ARE THE STAPLES OF THE PERSIAN CUISINE.

AND WHEN YOU COMBINE PERSIAN WITH VEGAN, THINGS GET EVEN BETTER. VEGAN DISHES ARE DELICIOUS ON THEIR OWN, RELYING MORE ON THE PURE FLAVORS OF VEGGIES, BUT THEN YOU ADD A TOUCH OF PERSIAN AND THE DISH IMPROVES ALL OF A SUDDEN, IT GETS EVEN MORE FLAVORFUL, IT GAINS MORE AROMA AND THE VEGGIES TURN INTO REAL DELICACIES INFUSED WITH SPICES OR FRESH HERBS.

Appetizers

Walnut and Cucumber Creamy Salad

VEGAN, CREAMY AND RICH ARE THE MAIN CHARACTERISTICS OF THIS SALAD. IT'S A DELICIOUS AND NUTRITIOUS SALAD THAT CAN BE SERVED IN INDIVIDUAL PORTIONS OR TOPPED ON SOME MINI FLATBREADS.

TIME: 30 MINUTES
SERVES: 2-4

INGREDIENTS:
1 CUP RAW CASHEWS, SOAKED OVER NIGHT
4 ICE CUBES, CRUSHED
3 CUCUMBERS, DICED
1 TABLESPOON CHOPPED PARSLEY
1 TEASPOON CHOPPED MINT
1 TEASPOON CHOPPED BASIL
½ CUP WALNUTS, CHOPPED
SALT, PEPPER TO TASTE
LEMON JUICE TO TASTE

DIRECTIONS:
1. COMBINE THE CASHEWS WITH THE ICE CUBES IN A BLENDER OR FOOD PROCESSOR AND PULSE UNTIL CREAMY AND SMOOTH.
2. SPOON THE MIXTURE INTO A BOWL AND STIR IN THE REST OF THE INGREDIENTS.
3. ADD SALT AND PEPPER TO TASTE AND GARNISH WITH LEMON JUICE TO TASTE.
4. SERVE THE SALAD WITH BREAD OR EVEN VEGETABLE STICKS.

Artichoke Heart Dip

TIME: 20 MINUTES
SERVES: 4-6

INGREDIENTS:
1 JAR ARTICHOKE HEARTS, DRAINED
3 GARLIC CLOVES
1 CUP FRESH SPINACH
½ CUP SOAKED CASHEW NUTS

SALT, PEPPER TO TASTE
½ LEMON, JUICED
2 TABLESPOONS OLIVE OIL
½ TEASPOON CAPERS
½ TEASPOON DRIED MINT

DIRECTIONS:
1. MIX ALL THE INGREDIENTS IN A BLENDER OR FOOD PROCESSOR.
2. PULSE UNTIL WELL BLENDED THEN SEASON WITH SALT AND PEPPER TO TASTE.
3. SPOON THE DIP INTO A SERVING BOWL AND SERVE WITH ANYTHING FROM CHIPS TO BREAD, CROUTONS OR VEGETABLE STICKS.

Baba Ganoush

BABA GANOUSH IS ONE OF THE MOST KNOWN PERSIAN FOODS AND IT COMBINES EGGPLANTS WITH TAHINI INTO AN EARTHY, FLAVORFUL AND RICH DIP THAT TASTES GREAT WITH TOASTED BREAD.

TIME: 1 HOUR
SERVES: 4-6

INGREDIENTS:
2 LARGE EGGPLANTS
2 TABLESPOONS TAHINI PASTE
4 GARLIC CLOVES, CHOPPED
2 TABLESPOONS CHOPPED CILANTRO
JUICE FROM ½ LEMON
¼ CUP OLIVE OIL
SALT, PEPPER TO TASTE

DIRECTIONS:
1. CUT THE EGGPLANTS IN HALF LENGTHWISE AND PLACE THEM ON A BAKING TRAY.
2. BAKE THE EGGPLANTS IN THE PREHEATED OVEN AT 375F FOR 30-40 MINUTES.
3. REMOVE FROM THE OVEN WHEN THE EGGPLANTS ARE SOFT.
4. SCOOP OUT THE SOFT, CREAMY FLESH AND PLACE IT IN A FOOD PROCESSOR.
5. LET IT COOL DOWN THEN ADD THE TAHINI PASTE, GARLIC, LEMON JUICE, OLIVE OIL, SALT AND PEPPER TO TASTE AND PROCESS UNTIL SMOOTH.
6. STIR IN THE CHOPPED CILANTRO AND SERVE THE BABA GANOUSH FRESH.

Green Avocado Dip on Toasted Bread

TIME: 25 MINUTES
SERVES: 4-6

INGREDIENTS:
1 RIPE AVOCADO, PEELED
JUICE FROM ½ LEMON
½ CUP CHOPPED CILANTRO
1 GREEN ONION, CHOPPED
1 GARLIC CLOVE, MINCED
SALT, PEPPER TO TASTE
2 TABLESPOONS SOAKED CASHEW NUTS
4-6 SLICES TOASTED BREAD

DIRECTIONS:
1. COMBINE THE AVOCADO WITH THE CASHEWS AND LEMON JUICE IN A BLENDER AND PULSE UNTIL CREAMY AND SMOOTH.
2. STIR IN THE CHOPPED CILANTRO, GREEN ONION AND GARLIC THEN SEASON WITH SALT AND PEPPER.
3. SPOON THE DIP ON TOASTED BREAD AND SERVE RIGHT AWAY.

Beet and Walnut Dip

TIME: 30 MINUTES
SERVES: 2-4

INGREDIENTS:
1 LARGE COOKED BEET, GRATED
1 CUP WALNUTS, CHOPPED
1 GARLIC CLOVE, MINCED
¼ CUP VEGAN MAYONNAISE
SALT, PEPPER TO TASTE
1 TABLESPOON LEMON JUICE
CRACKERS OR TOASTED BREAD FOR SERVING

DIRECTIONS:
1. COMBINE THE BEET WITH THE WALNUTS AND GARLIC THEN STIR IN THE MAYONNAISE, LEMON JUICE, SALT AND PEPPER.
2. SPOON THE SALAD INTO A BOWL AND SERVE IT WITH CRACKERS OR TOASTED BREAD.

Red Bell Pepper Hummus

UNLIKE THE TRADITIONAL HUMMUS, THIS RECIPE IS SWEETER AND HAS A SMOKY FLAVOR THAT MAKES IT SHINE. SO STEP OUT OF YOUR COMFORT ZONE AND TRY IT. YOU WILL LOVE IT!

TIME: 20 MINUTES
SERVES: 4-6

INGREDIENTS:
2 ROASTED RED BELL PEPPERS
1 CAN CHICKPEAS, DRAINED
4 GARLIC CLOVES
¼ CUP OLIVE OIL
JUICE FROM ½ LEMON

¼ CUP TAHINI PASTE
SALT, PEPPER TO TASTE
1 PINCH CHILI POWDER
MINI FLATBREAD TO SERVE

DIRECTIONS:
1. COMBINE ALL THE INGREDIENTS IN A FOOD PROCESSOR OR BLENDER AND PULSE UNTIL WELL BLENDED AND SMOOTH.
2. SPOON THE MIXTURE IN A SERVING BOWL AND SERVE IT WITH MINI FLATBREADS.

Eggplant and Tomato Fry Up

TIME: 25 MINUTES
SERVES: 2-4

INGREDIENTS:
1 EGGPLANT, PEELED AND DICED
1 RIPE TOMATO, DICED
2 GARLIC CLOVES, CHOPPED
1 TABLESPOON TOMATO PASTE
3 TABLESPOONS OLIVE OIL
SALT, PEPPER TO TASTE

DIRECTIONS:
1. HEAT THE OLIVE OIL IN A SKILLET AND STIR IN THE GARLIC.
2. SAUTÉ FOR 30 SECONDS THEN ADD THE EGGPLANT AND SAUTÉ FOR 10 MINUTES UNTIL GOLDEN BROWN AND TENDER.
3. STIR IN THE TOMATO PASTE THEN ADD THE DICED TOMATO, AS WELL AS SALT AND PEPPER.
4. COOK THE EGGPLANT FOR 10 MORE MINUTES, STIRRING OFTEN THEN TRANSFER IT IN A SERVING BOWL.
5. IT IS BEST SERVED WITH FLATBREAD.

Potato Creamy Salad

TIME: 30 MINUTES
SERVES: 4-6

INGREDIENTS:
6 COOKED RED POTATOES, DICED
2 PICKLED CUCUMBERS, DICED
1 GREEN ONION, CHOPPED
¼ TEASPOON GARLIC POWDER
½ CUP CASHEW NUTS, SOAKED IN WATER OVERNIGHT
2 TABLESPOONS LEMON JUICE
SALT, PEPPER TO TASTE
2 TABLESPOONS CHOPPED DILL
MINI FLATBREADS TO SERVE

DIRECTIONS:

1. MIX THE CASHEWS WITH THE LEMON JUICE IN A BOWL AND PULSE UNTIL SMOOTH.
2. COMBINE THE POTATOES WITH THE CUCUMBERS, ONION, GARLIC POWDER, DILL AND CASHEW SAUCE AND MIX GENTLY.
3. SEASON WITH SALT AND PEPPER AND SERVE RIGHT AWAY.

Tofu and Tomato Kebabs

THESE KEBABS ARE A CLASSIC. YOU WILL LOVE THEIR TASTE, BUT MOST OF ALL THE EASY TECHNIQUE THAT CAN BE APPLIED TO OTHER VEGGIES OR EVEN FRUITS AS WELL.

TIME: 15 MINUTES
SERVES: 4-6

INGREDIENTS:
2 CUPS CHERRY TOMATOES
6 OZ. TOFU, CUBED
4-6 WOODEN SKEWERS

DIRECTIONS:
1. PLACE THE TOMATOES AND TOFU ON SKEWERS, ALTERNATING ONE TOMATO WITH ONE CUBE OF CHEESE.
2. SERVE THE KEBABS FRESH.

Roasted Garlic Spread

DON'T UNDERESTIMATE THIS GARLIC SPREAD. IT HAS A DELICATE GARLIC FLAVOR AND IT'S SO FLAVORFUL THAT YOU WILL WANT MORE THAN ONE SERVING.

TIME: 1 HOUR 10 MINUTES
SERVES: 4-6

INGREDIENTS:
3 LARGE GARLIC HEADS
4 TABLESPOONS OLIVE OIL
1 TEASPOON SEA SALT
1 PINCH SMOKED PAPRIKA
¼ TEASPOON DRIED MINT

DIRECTIONS:
1. CUT THE GARLIC HEAD IN HALF HORIZONTALLY THEN WRAP EACH OF THEM IN ALUMINUM FOIL.
2. PLACE THEM ALL ON A BAKING TRAY AND ROAST IN THE PREHEATED OVEN AT 330F FOR 1 HOUR.
3. REMOVE FROM THE OVEN AND CAREFULLY UNWRAP EACH HALF OF GARLIC HEAD.
4. SQUEEZE OUT THE SOFT FLESH AND PLACE IT INTO A BOWL.
5. STIR IN THE SALT, PAPRIKA AND MINT AND MIX WELL.
6. SERVE IT WARM OR CHILLED, SPREAD ON BREAD, FLATBREAD OR EVEN CHIPS.

Salads
Orzo and Green Olive Salad

TIME: 40 MINUTES
SERVES: 4-6

INGREDIENTS:
1 CUP ORZO
2 CUPS WATER OR VEGETABLE STOCK
1 CUP SPINACH
2 TABLESPOONS PINE NUTS
4 BASIL LEAVES
4 MINT LEAVES
¼ CUP OLIVE OIL
SALT, PEPPER TO TASTE
¼ LEMON, JUICED
½ CUP CHOPPED GREEN OLIVES

DIRECTIONS:
1. MIX THE ORZO WITH THE WATER OR STOCK IN A SAUCEPAN AND COOK OVER MEDIUM FLAME UNTIL THE LIQUID IS ABSORBED. REMOVE FROM HEAT AND LET IT COOL DOWN.
2. COMBINE THE SPINACH WITH THE PINE NUTS, BASIL, MINT AND OLIVE OIL IN A BLENDER AND PULSE UNTIL SMOOTH.
3. SEASON WITH SALT AND PEPPER THEN ADD THE LEMON JUICE.
4. SPOON THE PESTO OVER THE COOKED ORZO AND MIX GENTLY.
5. SERVE THE SALAD RIGHT AWAY, TOPPED WITH GREEN OLIVES.

Fattoush Salad

THIS SALAD HAS BECOME A STAPLE OF THE PERSIAN CUISINE. IT IS A MIX OF VARIOUS VEGGIES AND IT HAS SUCH A FRESH AND DELICIOUS TASTE THAT YOU WILL KEEP ASKING FOR MORE.

TIME: 30 MINUTES
SERVES: 4-6

INGREDIENTS:
1 HEAD ROMAINE LETTUCE, SHREDDED
1 SHALLOT, SLICED
2 RIPE TOMATOES, SLICED
1 CUCUMBER, SLICED
¼ CUP BLACK OLIVES, CHOPPED

1 TABLESPOON CHOPPED MINT
½ CUP CHOPPED PARSLEY
1 TABLESPOON BALSAMIC VINEGAR
2 TABLESPOONS OLIVE OIL
1 TEASPOON SUMAC
¼ TEASPOON CUMIN POWDER
SALT, PEPPER TO TASTE
2 PITA BREADS, CUBED

DIRECTIONS:
1. COMBINE ALL THE VEGGIES IN A LARGE SALAD BOWL.
2. SPRINKLE WITH SALT, PEPPER, SUMAC AND CUMIN POWDER AND MIX GENTLY, ADDING THE VINEGAR AND OLIVE OIL AS WELL.
3. GENTLY STIR IN THE CUBED FLATBREAD AND SERVE RIGHT AWAY.

Persian Carrot Salad

TIME: 20 MINUTES
SERVES: 2-4

INGREDIENTS:
2 LARGE CARROTS, FINELY GRATED
½ CUP CASHEW NUTS, SOAKED OVERNIGHT
2 TABLESPOONS LEMON JUICE
2 TABLESPOONS ORANGE JUICE
¼ TEASPOON DRIED MINT
1 PINCH CHILI POWDER
SALT, PEPPER TO TASTE
¼ CUP SLICED ALMONDS

DIRECTIONS:
1. MIX THE CASHEW NUTS WITH THE LEMON JUICE AND ORANGE JUICE IN A BLENDER AND PULSE UNTIL WELL BLENDED.
2. TRANSFER THE MIXTURE INTO A BOWL AND STIR IN THE REST OF THE INGREDIENTS.
3. SERVE THE SALAD AS FRESH AS POSSIBLE.

Sumac Tomato Salad

SALADS PLAY AN IMPORTANT PART IN THE PERSIAN CUISINE THANKS TO ITS MEDITERRANEAN INFLUENCES. AND THIS SUMAC TOMATO SALAD IS A REAL DELICACY. DON'T SKIP THE SUMAC BECAUSE IT IS THE KEY INGREDIENT AND IT YIELDS A FRAGRANT SALAD TO BE SERVED AT ANY TIME OF THE DAY.

TIME: 25 MINUTES
SERVES: 4-6

INGREDIENTS:
4 RIPE TOMATOES, SLICED
1 RED ONION, SLICED
1 CUCUMBER, SLICED
1 CUP CHOPPED PARSLEY
2 TABLESPOONS LEMON JUICE
2 TABLESPOONS OLIVE OIL
1 TEASPOON SUMAC
SALT, PEPPER TO TASTE

DIRECTIONS:
1. COMBINE ALL THE INGREDIENTS IN A BOWL.
2. MIX GENTLY AND SERVE THE SALAD AS FRESH AS POSSIBLE.

Persian Chickpea Salad

TIME: 25 MINUTES
SERVES: 4-6

INGREDIENTS:
1 CAN CHICKPEAS, DRAINED
2 TABLESPOONS OLIVE OIL
½ TEASPOON CUMIN POWDER
1 GARLIC CLOVE, CHOPPED
½ TABLESPOON GRATED GINGER
1 LIME, JUICED
1 TOMATO, DICED
½ CUP CHOPPED CILANTRO
½ CUP CHOPPED PARSLEY

SALT, PEPPER TO TASTE

DIRECTIONS:
1. COMBINE ALL THE INGREDIENTS IN A SALAD BOWL.
2. SEASON WITH SALT AND PEPPER AND SERVE THE SALAD FRESH.

Shirazi Salad

TIME: 25 MINUTES
SERVES: 2-4

INGREDIENTS:
4 RIPE TOMATOES, DICED
2 CUCUMBERS, DICED
1 RED ONION, CHOPPED
1 TABLESPOON CHOPPED MINT
½ CUP CHOPPED PARSLEY
SALT, PEPPER TO TASTE
2 TABLESPOONS OLIVE OIL
1 LIME, JUICED
¼ TEASPOON SUMAC

DIRECTIONS:
1. COMBINE ALL THE INGREDIENTS IN A BOWL AND MIX GENTLY.
2. SERVE THE SALAD AS FRESH AS POSSIBLE.

Fresh Farro Salad

TIME: 30 MINUTES
SERVES: 4-6

INGREDIENTS:
1 CUP FARRO, RINSED
3 CUPS WATER
6 RADISHES, SLICED
2 CUCUMBERS, SLICED
2 TOMATOES, SLICED
½ CUP PITTED BLACK OLIVES
1 CUP CHOPPED PARSLEY
½ CUP CHOPPED CILANTRO
¼ CUP OLIVE OIL
SALT, PEPPER TO TASTE
1 LIME, JUICED
1 TEASPOON DRIED LIME

DIRECTIONS:
1. BRING THE WATER TO A BOIL WITH A PINCH OF SALT. STIR IN THE FARO AND COOK IT UNTIL THE LIQUID IS ABSORBED. REMOVE FROM HEAT AND LET IT COOL DOWN. FLUFF IT UP WITH A FORK AND TRANSFER IT INTO A BOWL.
2. STIR IN THE REST OF THE INGREDIENTS AND MIX GENTLY.
3. SERVE THE SALAD AS FRESH AS POSSIBLE.

Persian Rice and Cucumber Salad

TIME: 50 MINUTES
SERVES: 4-6

INGREDIENTS:
1 ½ CUPS PURPLE RICE
3 CUPS WATER
1 TEASPOON CORIANDER SEEDS
4 PERSIAN CUCUMBERS, SLICED
2 GREEN ONIONS, CHOPPED
1 CUP CHOPPED PARSLEY
¼ CUP CHOPPED MINT
3 TABLESPOONS OLIVE OIL
1 TEASPOON LEMON ZEST
2 TABLESPOONS LEMON JUICE
SALT, PEPPER TO TASTE

DIRECTIONS:
1. COMBINE THE RICE WITH THE WATER AND A PINCH OF SALT AND COOK UNTIL MOST OF THE LIQUID HAS BEEN ABSORBED. REMOVE FROM HEAT AND LET IT COOL DOWN THEN TRANSFER INTO A BOWL.
2. STIR IN THE CORIANDER SEEDS, CUCUMBERS, ONIONS, PARSLEY AND MINT.
3. ADD THE LEMON ZEST, OLIVE OIL AND LEMON JUICE THEN SEASON WITH SALT AND PEPPER TO TASTE.
4. MIX GENTLY AND SERVE THE SALAD AS FRESH AS POSSIBLE.

Soups and Stews
Persian Herb Soup

TIME: 40 MINUTES
SERVES: 4-6

INGREDIENTS:
2 TABLESPOONS OLIVE OIL
1 ONION, SLICED
3 GARLIC CLOVES, CHOPPED
1 CUP CANNED CHICKPEAS, DRAINED
1 CUP CANNED WHITE BEANS, DRAINED
1 TEASPOON TURMERIC POWDER
½ TEASPOON CUMIN POWDER
1 CUP CHOPPED PARSLEY
1 CUP CHOPPED CORIANDER
¼ CUP CHOPPED MINT
2 GREEN ONIONS, CHOPPED
2 CUPS BABY SPINACH, SHREDDED
SALT, PEPPER TO TASTE
4 CUPS WATER OR VEGETABLE STOCK

DIRECTIONS:
1. HEAT THE OLIVE OIL IN A SKILLET AND STIR IN THE ONION AND GARLIC. SAUTÉ FOR 2 MINUTES THEN ADD THE CHICKPEAS, BEANS, TURMERIC AND CUMIN POWDER.
2. POUR IN THE WATER AND ADD SALT AND PEPPER TO TASTE. COOK THE SOUP FOR 15 MINUTES THEN STIR IN THE HERBS, GREEN ONIONS AND SPINACH.
3. COOK FOR 15 MORE MINUTES THEN REMOVE FROM HEAT AND SERVE THE SOUP WARM.

Persian Mushroom Stew

TIME: 1 HOUR
SERVES: 4-6

INGREDIENTS:
3 TABLESPOONS VEGETABLE OIL
1 ONION, CHOPPED
2 GARLIC CLOVES, CHOPPED
2 POUNDS MUSHROOMS, SLICED
½ TEASPOON CUMIN POWDER
SALT, PEPPER TO TASTE
2 TABLESPOONS FLOUR
1 CUP ALMOND MILK

DIRECTIONS:
1. HEAT THE OIL IN A SKILLET AND STIR IN THE ONION AND GARLIC. SAUTÉ FOR 2 MINUTES THEN ADD THE MUSHROOMS.
2. LOWER THE HEAT AND COOK THE MUSHROOMS IN THEIR OWN JUICES FOR 10-15 MINUTES.
3. MIX WELL THE FLOUR WITH THE MILK AND POUR IT IN THE PAN OVER THE MUSHROOMS.
4. COOK UNTIL IT BEGINS TO THICKEN THEN ADJUST THE TASTE WITH SALT, PEPPER AND CUMIN POWDER.
5. REMOVE FROM HEAT AND SERVE IT WARM.

Persian Barley Soup – Ash-e-jow

BARLEY IS A GREAT ALTERNATIVE TO RICE OR OTHER KIND OF GRAIN. IT HAS A HIGH NUTRITIONAL CONTENT AND A NUTTY, EARTHY FLAVOR THAT WORKS GREAT IN SOUPS, AS WELL AS STEWS OR SALADS.

TIME: 40 MINUTES
SERVES: 4-6

INGREDIENTS:
2 TABLESPOONS OLIVE OIL
1 ONION, CHOPPED
1 GARLIC CLOVE, CHOPPED
1 CUP UNCOOKED BARLEY, RINSED
4 CUPS VEGETABLE STOCK
½ TEASPOON TURMERIC POWDER
½ TEASPOON CUMIN POWDER
1 LIME, JUICED
2 TOMATOES, DICED
1 CARROT, DICED
SALT, PEPPER TO TASTE
2 TABLESPOONS CHOPPED PARSLEY

DIRECTIONS:
1. HEAT THE OLIVE OIL IN A SOUP POT AND STIR IN THE ONION AND GARLIC. SAUTÉ FOR 2 MINUTES THEN ADD THE BARLEY, TURMERIC AND CUMIN.
2. SAUTÉ FOR 2 MORE MINUTES THEN STIR IN THE TOMATOES AND CARROT.
3. POUR IN THE STOCK THEN SEASON WITH SALT AND PEPPER AND COOK FOR 20-30 MINUTES ON LOW HEAT.
4. WHEN DONE, REMOVE FROM HEAT AND

STIR IN THE CHOPPED PARSLEY.
5. SERVE THE SOUP WARM AND FRESH.

Pomegranate Soup

ALTHOUGH SLIGHTLY UNUSUAL, THIS SOUP IS A TANGY DELICACY. IF YOU LIKE BOLD FOODS, THIS IS THE ONE FOR YOU.

TIME: 1 HOUR
SERVES: 4-6

INGREDIENTS:
2 CUPS VEGETABLE STOCK
4 CUPS WATER
½ TEASPOON TURMERIC POWDER
1 CUP SHORT GRAIN RICE, RINSED
2 BEETS, GRATED
1 CUP POMEGRANATE JUICE
½ CUP CHOPPED PARSLEY
½ CUP CHOPPED CILANTRO
1 TEASPOON DRIED MINT
SALT, PEPPER TO TASTE

DIRECTIONS:
1. COMBINE THE WATER WITH THE STOCK, RICE, TURMERIC AND BEETS IN A SOUP POT.
2. ADD SALT AND PEPPER TO TASTE AND COOK FOR 20-30 MINUTES.
3. STIR IN THE REST OF THE INGREDIENTS AND COOK 10 MORE MINUTES.
4. REMOVE FROM HEAT AND LET IT COOL DOWN BEFORE SERVING.

Cold Cucumber Soup

TIME: 20 MINUTES
SERVES: 2-4

INGREDIENTS:
2 LARGE CUCUMBERS
1 CUP CASHEW NUTS, SOAKED OVERNIGHT
½ CUP CRUSHED ICE
½ CUP WATER
2 GARLIC CLOVES
½ LEMON, JUICED
2 TABLESPOONS OLIVE OIL FOR SERVING

1 TABLESPOON CHOPPED DILL
SALT, PEPPER TO TASTE

DIRECTIONS:
1. COMBINE THE CUCUMBERS WITH THE CASHEWS, ICE, WATER, GARLIC AND LEMON JUICE IN A BLENDER. ADD THE DILL AND PULSE AGAIN.
2. ADD SALT AND PEPPER TO TASTE AND PULSE UNTIL WELL BLENDED AND SMOOTH.
3. TOP WITH A DRIZZLE OF OLIVE OIL BEFORE SERVING.

Persian Pistachio Soup

TIME: 1 HOUR
SERVES: 4-6

INGREDIENTS:
1 CUP SHELLED PISTACHIO
2 TABLESPOONS OLIVE OIL
1 SHALLOT, CHOPPED
1 LEEK, CHOPPED
2 GARLIC CLOVES, CHOPPED
2 TABLESPOONS ALL PURPOSE FLOUR
6 CUPS VEGETABLE STOCK
2 TABLESPOONS LEMON JUICE
SALT, PEPPER TO TASTE
2 TABLESPOONS CHOPPED CILANTRO

DIRECTIONS:
1. GROUND THE PISTACHIO IN A FOOD PROCESSOR AND SET ASIDE.
2. HEAT THE OIL IN A SOUP POT AND STIR IN THE SHALLOT, GARLIC AND LEEK. SAUTÉ FOR 5 MINUTES THEN STIR IN THE FLOUR.
3. POUR IN THE STOCK THEN STIR IN THE PISTACHIO AND LEMON JUICE.
4. ADD SALT AND PEPPER TO TASTE AND COOK THE SOUP FOR 40 MINUTES ON LOW HEAT.
5. PUREE THE SOUP WITH AN IMMERSION BLENDER.
6. SERVE THE SOUP FRESH, TOPPED WITH CHOPPED CILANTRO.

Persian Herbed Bean Soup

TIME: 1 HOUR
SERVES: 4-6

INGREDIENTS:
2 TABLESPOONS OLIVE OIL
1 LARGE ONION, CHOPPED
2 GARLIC CLOVES, CHOPPED
3 CUPS CANNED KIDNEY BEANS, DRAINED
1 TEASPOON TURMERIC
4 CUPS WATER
1 CUP VEGETABLE STOCK
1 CUP CHOPPED PARSLEY
1 CUP CHOPPED CILANTRO
1 CUP CHOPPED CHIVES
SALT, PEPPER TO TASTE
1 LIME, JUICED

DIRECTIONS:
1. HEAT THE OLIVE OIL IN A SOUP POT AND STIR IN THE ONION AND GARLIC. SAUTÉ FOR 2 MINUTES THEN STIR IN THE BEANS, TURMERIC, WATER AND STOCK.
2. COOK THE BEANS FOR 15 MINUTES THEN STIR IN THE HERBS.
3. SEASON WITH SALT AND PEPPER TO TASTE AND COOK 15-20 MORE MINUTES.
4. GARNISH THE SOUP WITH LIME JUICE AND SERVE IT WARM AND FRESH.

Tofu Spinach Soup

TIME: 45 MINUTES
SERVES: 4-6

INGREDIENTS:
10 OZ FIRM TOFU, CUBED
3 TABLESPOONS VEGETABLE OIL
1 TEASPOON TURMERIC POWDER
1 LARGE ONION, FINELY CHOPPED
4 GARLIC CLOVES, CHOPPED
2 CUPS CANNED KIDNEY BEANS, DRAINED
4 CUPS VEGETABLE STOCK
4 CUPS FRESH SPINACH, SHREDDED
1 CUP CHOPPED PARSLEY
½ CUP CHOPPED CORIANDER
SALT, PEPPER TO TASTE
1 LIME, JUICED

DIRECTIONS:
1. HEAT THE OIL IN A SOUP POT AND STIR IN THE TOFU. SAUTÉ FOR 5 MINUTES UNTIL GOLDEN BROWN ON ALL SIDES THEN STIR IN THE TURMERIC POWDER, ONION AND GARLIC.
2. SAUTÉ FOR 5 MORE MINUTES, STIRRING OFTEN THEN ADD THE BEANS AND STOCK.
3. SEASON WITH SALT AND PEPPER AND COOK THE SOUP FOR 25 MINUTES.
4. STIR IN THE PARSLEY, CORIANDER AND SPINACH AND COOK FOR 15 MORE MINUTES.
5. GARNISH THE SOUP WITH LIME JUICE THEN REMOVE IT FROM HEAT AND LET IT COOL DOWN SLIGHTLY.
6. SERVE THE SOUP FRESH.

Bean and Mushroom Stew

TIME: 1 HOUR
SERVES: 4-6

INGREDIENTS:
2 TABLESPOONS VEGETABLE OIL
1 ONION, SLICED
4 GARLIC CLOVES, CHOPPED
2 POUNDS MUSHROOMS, SLICED
2 CUPS CANNED BLACK BEANS, DRAINED
1 CUP TOMATO PUREE
1 CUP VEGETABLE STOCK
1 TEASPOON TURMERIC POWDER
¼ TEASPOON CAYENNE PEPPER
2 SWEET POTATOES, PEELED AND CUBED
SALT, PEPPER TO TASTE
¼ CUP CHOPPED CILANTRO

DIRECTIONS:
1. HEAT THE OIL IN A HEAVY SAUCEPAN AND STIR IN THE ONION AND GARLIC. SAUTÉ FOR 2 MINUTES THEN ADD THE MUSHROOMS, BEANS, TURMERIC, CAYENNE PEPPER AND SWEET POTATOES.
2. SAUTÉ FOR 5 MORE MINUTES THEN POUR IN THE TOMATO PUREE AND STOCK.
3. SEASON WITH SALT AND PEPPER TO TASTE AND COOK THE SOUP OVER MEDIUM FLAME FOR 30-40 MINUTES.
4. WHEN DONE, REMOVE FROM HEAT AND STIR IN THE CILANTRO.
5. SERVE THE STEW WARM AND FRESH.

Rhubarb Stew

YES, YOU READ THAT RIGHT! A SAVORY STEW WITH RHUBARB! YOU WILL BE SURPRISED TO DISCOVER A TANGY, DELICATE STEW THAT OFFERS A GREAT EXPERIENCE FOR A BOLD PALATE.

TIME: 1 HOUR
SERVES: 2-4

INGREDIENTS:
1 ONION, FINELY CHOPPED
1 LARGE CARROT, SLICED
1 CUP WATER
3 CUPS CHOPPED PARSLEY
1 TEASPOON TURMERIC POWDER
½ TEASPOON SAFFRON STRANDS
1 POUND FRESH RHUBARB, CUT INTO 1-INCH PIECES
SALT, PEPPER TO TASTE
COOKED RICE FOR SERVING

DIRECTIONS:
1. COMBINE THE ONION, WATER AND CARROT IN A SAUCEPAN. COOK FOR 10 MINUTES THEN ADD THE TURMERIC, SAFFRON AND RHUBARB.
2. LOWER THE HEAT AND COOK THE STEW FOR 15-20 MINUTES.
3. ADD SALT AND PEPPER TO TASTE THEN STIR IN THE PARSLEY.
COOK 10 MORE MINUTES THEN REMOVE FROM HEAT AND SERVE THE STEW WARM WITH COOKED RICE.

Persian Eggplant Stew

EGGPLANTS ARE HIGHLY USED IN THE PERSIAN CUISINE AND THE TRUTH IS THAT ALL THE DISHES USING THEM ARE FLAVORFUL AND DELICIOUS. THESE SUMMER VEGETABLES CAN BECOME REAL DELICACIES IF COOKED FOLLOWING A PERSIAN RECIPE.

TIME: 1 HOUR
SERVES: 4-6
INGREDIENTS:
2 ONIONS, CHOPPED
4 TABLESPOONS OLIVE OIL

2 GARLIC CLOVES, CHOPPED
2 LARGE EGGPLANTS, PEELED AND CUBED
2 RIPE TOMATOES, DICED
½ TEASPOON CUMIN POWDER
1 TEASPOON TURMERIC
1 CUP TOMATO SAUCE
1 CUP VEGETABLE STOCK
SALT, PEPPER TO TASTE
DIRECTIONS:
1. HEAT THE OIL IN A SKILLET AND STIR IN THE ONIONS AND GARLIC. SAUTÉ FOR 5-7 MINUTES.
2. STIR IN THE EGGPLANTS AND TOMATOES, AS WELL AS CUMIN POWDER AND TURMERIC AND SAUTÉ FOR 5 MORE MINUTES.
3. ADD THE STOCK AND TOMATO SAUCE THEN SEASON WITH SALT AND PEPPER TO TASTE. LOWER THE HEAT AND COOK THE STEW FOR 30 MINUTES.
4. SERVE THE STEW WARM AND FRESH.

Persian Celery and Potato Stew

TIME: 1 HOUR
SERVES: 4-6

INGREDIENTS:
4 TABLESPOONS VEGETABLE OIL
3 CELERY STALKS, CHOPPED
1 ONION, CHOPPED
2 GARLIC CLOVES, CHOPPED
1 TEASPOON DRIED MINT
½ TEASPOON TURMERIC
2 CUPS TOMATO PUREE
1 CUP VEGETABLE STOCK
1 BAY LEAF
1 ½ POUNDS POTATOES, PEELED AND CUBED
SALT, PEPPER TO TASTE
1 LIME, JUICED

DIRECTIONS:
1. HEAT THE OIL IN A SOUP POT AND STIR IN THE CELERY, POTATOES, ONION AND GARLIC.
2. SAUTÉ FOR 5-10 MINUTES, STIRRING OFTEN THEN ADD THE DRIED MINT AND TURMERIC.
3. POUR IN THE TOMATO PUREE AND STOCK THEN ADD THE BAY LEAF, SALT AND PEPPER TO TASTE.
4. COOK THE STEW FOR 30-40 MINUTES UNTIL THE POTATOES ARE TENDER.
5. ADD THE LIME JUICE AND SERVE THE STEW WARM.

Lentil and Beet Soup with Flour Dumplings

TIME: 1 HOUR
SERVES: 4-6

INGREDIENTS:
SOUP:
1 CUP LENTILS, RINSED
2 MEDIUM SIZE BEETROOTS, GRATED
1 ONION, CHOPPED
5 CUPS VEGETABLE STOCK
½ TEASPOON DRIED MINT
½ CUP CHOPPED DILL
½ CUP CHOPPED PARSLEY
½ TEASPOON TURMERIC
SALT, PEPPER TO TASTE
1 LIME, JUICED
DUMPLINGS:
½ CUP ALL PURPOSE FLOUR
¼ CUP WARM WATER

DIRECTIONS:
1. TO MAKE THE SOUP, COMBINE ALL THE INGREDIENTS IN A SOUP BOWL AND COOK ON LOW HEAT UNTIL THE LENTILS ARE COOKED THROUGH, AROUND 30 MINUTES.
2. SEASON THE SOUP WITH SALT AND PEPPER.
3. TO MAKE THE DUMPLINGS, COMBINE THE FLOUR WITH THE WATER.
4. DROP PIECES OF DOUGH IN THE BOILING SOUP AND COOK JUST 5-7 MORE MINUTES.
REMOVE FROM HEAT AND LET IT COOL DOWN SLIGHTLY BEFORE SERVING.

Eggplant and Green Grape Stew

THIS STEW WILL SURPRISE YOU FOR SURE. IT IS RICH AND FLAVORFUL, BUT THE GRAPES CUT DOWN THROUGH THAT RICHNESS WITH THEIR DELICATE TANGINESS. OVERALL, IT IS A BALANCED AND DELICIOUS STEW THAT WILL MAKE YOU STEP OUT OF YOUR COMFORT ZONE.

TIME: 1 HOUR
SERVES: 4-6

INGREDIENTS:
3 EGGPLANTS, PEELED AND DICED
2 GARLIC CLOVES, CHOPPED
1 SHALLOT, SLICED
4 TABLESPOONS OLIVE OIL
1 TEASPOON DRIED MINT
½ TEASPOON SUMAC
1 CUP SEEDLESS GRAPES
SALT, PEPPER TO TASTE
4 RIPE TOMATOES, SLICED

DIRECTIONS:
1. HEAT THE OIL IN A SKILLET AND STIR IN THE GARLIC AND SHALLOT. SAUTÉ FOR 2 MINUTES THEN ADD THE MIN, SUMAC AND EGGPLANT.
2. SAUTÉ FOR 5-10 MINUTES THEN ADD THE GRAPES AND TOMATOES.
3. SEASON WITH SALT AND PEPPER THEN LOWER THE HEAT AND COOK THE STEW IN ITS OWN JUICE FOR 30-40 MINUTES. IF NEEDED, ADD A BIT OF WATER.
4. WHEN DONE, REMOVE FROM HEAT AND LET IT COOL DOWN COMPLETELY BEFORE SERVING.

Main Dishes
Veggie Stuffed Bell Peppers

THIS VERSATILE RECIPE IS A GREAT CHOICE FOR LUNCH OR DINNER. THE PEPPERS CAN BE MADE AHEAD OF TIME, COOKED THEN FROZEN AND JUST REHEATED WHEN YOU WANT SOME PERSIAN FLAVORS FLOODING YOUR SENSES.

TIME: 1 ½ HOURS
SERVES: 6

INGREDIENTS:

6 GREEN OR RED BELL PEPPERS
4 CARROTS, GRATED
2 ONIONS, CHOPPED
4 TABLESPOONS OLIVE OIL
1 CUP RICE, RINSED
½ CUP TOMATO PASTE
1 CUP CHOPPED PARSLEY
1 CUP CHOPPED CILANTRO
1 TEASPOON DRIED MINT
1 TEASPOON DRIED THYME
¼ TEASPOON CUMIN POWDER
SALT, PEPPER TO TASTE
2 CUPS VEGETABLE STOCK
1 CUP TOMATO PUREE
1 BAY LEAF

DIRECTIONS:
1. CUT THE TOP OF EACH BELL PEPPER AND REMOVE THE CORE. SET ASIDE.
2. HEAT THE OIL IN A SKILLET AND STIR IN THE CARROTS AND ONIONS. SAUTÉ FOR 10 MINUTES THEN ADD THE RICE AND TOMATO PASTE.
3. MIX WELL AND COOK 5 MORE MINUTE THEN REMOVE FROM HEAT AND STIR IN THE PARSLEY, CILANTRO, MINT, THYME AND CUMIN POWDER.
4. SEASON WITH SALT AND PEPPER THEN FILL EACH PEPPER WITH THIS MIXTURE.
5. PLACE THEM ALL IN A SOUP POT AND POUR IN THE STOCK AND TOMATO PUREE.
6. ADD THE BAY LEAF, A PINCH OF SALT AND COOK ON LOW HEAT FOR 1 HOUR.
7. SERVE THE PEPPERS WARM.

Persian Potato Gratin

TIME: 1 ½ HOURS
SERVES: 6-8

INGREDIENTS:
2 POUND RED POTATOES, PEELED AND FINELY SLICED
10 OZ. CREAMY TOFU
1 CUP ALMOND MILK
2 TABLESPOONS COCONUT OIL
1 TEASPOON DRIED MINT
½ TEASPOON DRIED THYME
½ TEASPOON DRIED OREGANO
1 TEASPOON GARLIC POWDER
SALT, PEPPER TO TASTE

DIRECTIONS:
1. COMBINE THE TOFU WITH THE MILK, COCONUT OIL, HERBS AND GARLIC POWDER IN A BLENDER AND PULSE UNTIL SMOOTH.
2. ADD SALT AND PEPPER TO TASTE IF NEEDED.
3. IN A SMALL DEEP DISH BAKING PAN, LAYER THE THIN POTATO SLICES WITH THE TOFU MIXTURE, FINISHING WITH A LAYER OF TOFU.
4. BAKE THE GRATIN IN THE PREHEATED OVEN AT 350F FOR 40-50 MINUTES UNTIL TENDER AND FRAGRANT.
5. SERVE THE POTATOES WARM.

Potato and Prune Casserole

THIS IS DEFINITELY NOT YOUR USUAL CASSEROLE, BUT DON'T AVOID IT! DRIED PRUNES ARE A GREAT SOURCE OF NUTRIENTS AND FLAVOR, ESPECIALLY IF YOU CAN FIND THE SMOKED ONES.

TIME: 1 HOUR
SERVES: 4-6

INGREDIENTS:
2 POUNDS RED POTATOES, PEELED AND CUBED
2 CUPS PITTED PRUNES, COARSELY CHOPPED
1 ONION, CHOPPED
2 TABLESPOONS OLIVE OIL
2 GARLIC CLOVES, CHOPPED
SALT, PEPPER TO TASTE
2 CUPS TOMATO SAUCE
½ TEASPOON CUMIN POWDER
1 PINCH CHILI FLAKES
½ TEASPOON SAFFRON

DIRECTIONS:
1. HEAT THE OLIVE OIL IN A FRYING PAN AND STIR IN THE ONION AND GARLIC. SAUTÉ FOR 2 MINUTES THEN ADD THE POTATOES AND PRUNES.
2. SAUTÉ FOR 10 MINUTES, STIRRING IN THE CUMIN POWDER, CHILI AND SAFFRON.
3. TRANSFER THE MIXTURE IN A DEEP DISH BAKING PAN AND POUR THE TOMATO SAUCE OVER THE POTATOES.
4. COOK IN THE PREHEATED OVEN AT 350F FOR 40-50 MINUTES.
5. REMOVE FROM HEAT WHEN DONE AND SERVE WARM.

Kateh – Persian Rice

TIME: 10 MINUTES
SERVES: 4-6

INGREDIENTS:
4 CUPS COOKED BASMATI RICE
2 TABLESPOONS VEGETABLE OIL
1 TEASPOON DRIED MINT
SALT, PEPPER TO TASTE

DIRECTIONS:
1. HEAT THE OIL IN A SKILLET. STIR IN THE RICE AND FRY IT A FEW MINUTES, STIRRING OFTEN.
2. ADD THE MINT AND SEASON WITH SALT AND PEPPER.
3. SERVE THE RICE WARM.

Pomegranate Roasted Tofu

INFUSED WITH POMEGRANATE JUICE TOFU TURNS INTO A DELICATE AND DELICIOUS ROAST THAT CAN BE SERVED WITH ANY SIDE DISH YOU LIKE.

TIME: 45 MINUTES
SERVES: 4

INGREDIENTS:
4 THICK SLICES TOFU
1 CUP POMEGRANATE JUICE
1 TABLESPOON SOY SAUCE
1 SHALLOT, CHOPPED
4 TABLESPOONS OLIVE OIL
1 PINCH BLACK PEPPER

DIRECTIONS:
1. COMBINE THE POMEGRANATE JUICE WITH THE SOY SAUCE AND SHALLOT IN A BOWL.
2. ADD THE TOFU SLICES AND LET THEM MARINATE FOR 30 MINUTES AT LEAST.
3. DRAIN THEM AND PLACE THEM ON A BAKING TRAY.
4. SPRINKLE WITH BLACK PEPPER AND DRIZZLE WITH OIL.
5. ROAST THE TOFU IN THE PREHEATED OVEN AT 400F FOR 15-20 MINUTES.
6. SERVE IT WARM WITH YOUR FAVORITE SIDE DISH.

Saffron Baked Mushrooms

TIME: 40 MINUTES
SERVES: 6

INGREDIENTS:
6 PORTOBELLO MUSHROOMS
1 ONION, FINELY CHOPPED
2 TABLESPOONS OLIVE OIL
2 GARLIC CLOVES, CHOPPED
1 CUP GROUND ALMONDS
1 TEASPOON DRIED MINT
SALT, PEPPER TO TASTE
½ TEASPOON SAFFRON

DIRECTIONS:
1. HEAT THE OIL IN A SKILLET AND STIR IN THE ONION AND GARLIC. SAUTÉ FOR 2 MINUTES THEN REMOVE FROM HEAT AND ADD THE GROUND ALMONDS, SAFFRON AND MINT.
2. SEASON WITH SALT AND PEPPER THEN SPOON THE MIXTURE INTO EACH MUSHROOM CAP.
3. PLACE THEM ALL ON A BAKING TRAY AND BAKE IN THE PREHEATED OVEN AT 350F FOR 30 MINUTES.
4. LET THEM COOL DOWN A FEW MINUTES BEFORE SERVING.

Walnut and Rice Balls

IT'S NOT UNUSUAL FOR THE PERSIAN CUISINE TO USE WALNUTS OR OTHER KIND OF NUTS. BUT EVEN MORE UNUSUAL IS THAT THESE NUTS ARE BEING USED IN SAVORY FOODS, SUCH AS THESE RICE BALLS.

TIME: 1 HOUR
SERVES: 8

INGREDIENTS:
4 CUPS COOKED SHORT GRAIN RICE
1 CUP GROUND WALNUTS
¼ CUP CHICKPEA FLOUR
¼ CUP CHOPPED PARSLEY
1 TABLESPOON CHOPPED TARRAGON
1 TEASPOON DRIED MINT
1 TEASPOON TURMERIC POWDER
½ TEASPOON CUMIN POWDER
SALT, PEPPER TO TASTE
WATER TO COOK THEM

DIRECTIONS:
1. POUR A FEW CUPS OF WATER IN A LARGE POT AND BRING TO A BOIL WITH A PINCH OF SALT. LET IT COME TO A BOIL WHILE YOU MAKE THE RICE BALLS.
2. COMBINE THE RICE WITH THE REST OF THE INGREDIENTS IN A LARGE BOWL. SEASON WITH SALT AND PEPPER THEN WET YOUR HANDS AND FORM MEDIUM SIZE BALLS.
3. DROP THEM ALL IN THE HOT, BOILING WATER TRYING NOT TO CROWD THEM. AT FIRST THEY WILL SINK BUT AS THEY COOK THEY WILL COME TO THE SURFACE. AFTER 3-4 MINUTES THEY ARE DONE. CAREFULLY DRAIN THEM AND

SERVE THEM AS MAIN DISH OR SIDE DISH.

Persian Pilaf

PILAF IS A RICE DISH BUT IT'S VERSATILE AND RICH, PERFECT FOR LUNCH OR DINNER AND SUITED FOR THE ENTIRE FAMILY.

TIME: 1 HOUR
SERVES: 4-6

INGREDIENTS:
2 TABLESPOONS OLIVE OIL
1 SHALLOT CHOPPED
1 CARROT, DICED
½ CELERY STALK, DICED
½ CUP RAISINS

1 TEASPOON DRIED MINT
1 TEASPOON GRATED GINGER
1 TEASPOON TURMERIC
1 CUP SHORT GRAIN RICE, RINSED
3 CUPS VEGETABLE STOCK

DIRECTIONS:
1. HEAT THE OIL IN A HEAVY SAUCEPAN AND STIR IN THE SHALLOT, CARROT AND CELERY. SAUTÉ FOR 2 MINUTES THEN STIR IN THE RAISINS, MINT, GINGER, TURMERIC AND RICE.
2. SAUTÉ FOR 2 MORE MINUTES THEN ADD THE STOCK.
3. LOWER THE HEAT, COVER WITH A LID AND COOK THE PILAF FOR 30 MINUTES UNTIL MOST OF THE LIQUID HAS BEEN ABSORBED.
4. REMOVE FROM HEAT AND SERVE THE PILAF WARM.

Vegetable Curry

THE GREAT THING ABOUT THIS RECIPE IS THAT YOU CAN USE ANY VEGETABLES YOU WANT AND IT WILL STILL TASTE GREAT AND BE RICH AND FLAVORFUL.

TIME: 1 HOUR
SERVES: 4-6

INGREDIENTS:
1 ONION, CHOPPED
2 GARLIC CLOVES, CHOPPED
2 TABLESPOONS VEGETABLE OIL
1 LARGE CARROT, SLICED
1 POUND RED POTATOES, PEELED AND CUBED
1 POUND SWEET POTATOES, PEELED AND CUBED
2 TABLESPOONS CURRY PASTE
1 TEASPOON TURMERIC POWDER
1 CUP VEGETABLE STOCK
1 CUP COCONUT MILK
SALT, PEPPER TO TASTE
1 BAY LEAF

DIRECTIONS:
1. HEAT THE OIL IN A HEAVY SAUCEPAN AND STIR IN THE ONION AND GARLIC. SAUTÉ FOR 2 MINUTES UNTIL SOFT AND TRANSLUCENT THEN STIR IN THE CARROT AND POTATOES.
2. SAUTÉ FOR 5 MINUTES, STIRRING OFTEN, THEN ADD THE CURRY PASTE, TURMERIC POWDER, STOCK AND COCONUT MILK.
3. ADD SALT AND PEPPER TO TASTE, AS WELL AS ONE BAY LEAF AND COOK THE CURRY ON LOW TO MEDIUM HEAT FOR 30-40 MINUTES UNTIL THE VEGGIES ARE TENDER.
4. REMOVE FROM HEAT AND SERVE THE

CURRY WARM.

Fried Eggplant Casserole

TIME: 1 HOUR
SERVES: 4-6

INGREDIENTS:
2 LARGE EGGPLANTS, PEELED AND CUBED
¼ CUP VEGETABLE OIL
1 CAN DICED TOMATOES
½ CUP TOMATO JUICE
1 TEASPOON DRIED MINT
1 TEASPOON DRIED BASIL
½ TEASPOON GROUND GINGER
SALT, PEPPER TO TASTE

DIRECTIONS:
1. HEAT THE OIL IN A SKILLET AND STIR IN THE EGGPLANT.
2. FRY FOR 10 MINUTES, STIRRING OFTEN THEN ADD THE REST OF THE INGREDIENTS.
3. SEASON WITH SALT AND PEPPER AND TRANSFER THE EGGPLANT IN A DEEP DISH BAKING PAN.
4. BAKE THE EGGPLANT IN THE PREHEATED OVEN AT 350F FOR 20-30 MINUTES.
5. SERVE THE CASSEROLE WARM.

Falafel Loaf

FALAFEL HAS A BALL SHAPE USUALLY BUT IT CAN TIME CONSUMING SHAPED LIKE THAT. THIS VERSION IS MUCH EASIER BECAUSE THE MIXTURE IS BAKED IN A LOAF PAN AND THE RESULT IS A FLAVORFUL AND DELICIOUS LOAF THAT CAN BE EVEN FROZEN FOR LATER SERVING IF YOU WANT.

TIME: 1 ¼ HOURS
SERVES: 6-8

INGREDIENTS:
2 CANS CHICKPEAS, DRAINED
1 CUP TOMATO SAUCE
½ CUP GROUND FLAX SEEDS
½ CUP COLD WATER
1 POUND BABY CARROTS, DICED
1 ONION, FINELY CHOPPED
4 GARLIC CLOVES, CHOPPED
1 CUP CHOPPED PARSLEY
SALT, PEPPER TO TASTE
¼ CUP OLIVE OIL

DIRECTIONS:
1. PLACE THE CHICKPEAS IN A FOOD PROCESSOR AND PULSE UNTIL GROUND.
2. IN A BOWL, COMBINE THE GROUND FLAX SEEDS WITH THE WATER AND LET THEM SOAK 10 MINUTES.
3. STIR IN THE CHICKPEAS, TOMATO SAUCE, CARROTS, ONION, GARLIC AND PARSLEY.
4. ADD SALT AND PEPPER TO TASTE AND MIX WELL THEN STIR IN THE OLIVE OIL AND SPOON THE MIXTURE INTO A LOAF PAN LINED WITH

PARCHMENT PAPER.
5. BAKE THE FALAFEL LOAF IN THE PREHEATED OVEN AT 350F FOR 40 MINUTES.
6. REMOVE FROM THE OVEN AND LET IT COOL DOWN BEFORE SERVING.

Persian Okra Stew

TIME: 1 HOUR
SERVES: 6-8

INGREDIENTS:
3 TABLESPOONS VEGETABLE OIL
1 ONION, CHOPPED
2 GARLIC CLOVES, CHOPPED
1 CARROT, DICED
2 POUND OKRA, TRIMMED AND HALVED
1 CUP DICED TOMATOES
1 CUP TOMATO PUREE
1 TEASPOON DRIED MINT
½ TEASPOON DRIED THYME
SALT, PEPPER TO TASTE
2 TABLESPOONS CHOPPED PARSLEY
2 TABLESPOONS CHOPPED CILANTRO

DIRECTIONS:
1. HEAT THE OIL IN A SAUCEPAN AND STIR IN THE ONION, GARLIC AND CARROT.
2. SAUTÉ FOR 2-3 MINUTES THEN ADD THE OKRA, TOMATOES AND TOMATO PUREE.
3. STIR IN THE MINT AND THYME THEN SEASON WITH SALT AND PEPPER TO TASTE.
4. COOK THE STEW FOR 30-40 MINUTES ON LOW HEAT.
5. WHEN DONE, REMOVE THE STEW FROM HEAT AND STIR IN THE CHOPPED HERBS.
6. SERVE IT WARM AND FRESH.

Persian Veggie Cabbage Rolls

CABBAGE ROLLS CAN BE FOUND IN MANY PARTS OF THE GLOBE, BUT NONE OF THEM TASTES AS FRESH AND BOLD AS THESE ONES.

TIME: 1 ½ HOURS
SERVES: 8-10

INGREDIENTS:
1 LARGE CABBAGE
4 TABLESPOONS VEGETABLE OIL
2 ONIONS, FINELY CHOPPED
1 LARGE CARROT, FINELY CHOPPED
2 GARLIC CLOVES, CHOPPED
1 CELERY STALK, CHOPPED
1 CUP SHORT GRAIN RICE, RINSED
1 CUP CANNED CHICKPEAS, DRAINED
1 CUP CHOPPED PARSLEY
1 CUP CHOPPED CILANTRO
¼ CUP CHOPPED MINT
2 GREEN ONIONS, CHOPPED
SALT, PEPPER TO TASTE
1 LEMON, JUICED
4 CUPS WATER
1 TEASPOON DRIED THYME
1 BAY LEAF

DIRECTIONS:
1. HEAT THE OIL IN A SKILLET AND STIR IN THE ONIONS, CARROT, GARLIC AND CELERY.
2. SAUTÉ FOR 10 MINUTES, STIRRING OFTEN, THEN ADD THE RICE AND COOK 5 MORE MINUTES.
3. REMOVE FROM HEAT AND STIR IN THE CHOPPED HERBS, CHICKPEAS AND GREEN

ONIONS.
4. ADD SALT AND PEPPER TO TASTE AND LET THE MIXTURE COOL DOWN.
5. CAREFULLY PEEL THE CABBAGE, LEAF BY LEAF AND SET ASIDE.
6. POUR A FEW CUPS OF WATER IN A LARGE POT AND BRING TO A BOIL. THROW IN THE CABBAGE LEAVES AND COOK THEM JUST A FEW MINUTES TO SOFTEN THEM.
7. DRAIN AND LET THEM COOL DOWN.
8. TO FINISH THE ROLLS, TAKE ONE LEAF OF CABBAGE AND PLACE A FEW SPOONS OF VEGGIE FILLING AT ONE END OF THE LEAF. CAREFULLY ROLL THE LEAF TIGHTLY AND SECURE THE ENDS BY PUSHING THEM INTO THE ROLL.
9. PLACE ALL THE ROLLS IN A SAUCEPAN.
10. POUR IN THE WATER, ADD THE THYME AND BAY LEAF AND A PINCH OF SALT AND COOK THE CABBAGE ROLLS FOR 1 HOUR OR EVEN MORE AT LOW HEAT.
11. SERVE THE ROLLS WARM.

Couscous Stuffed Tomatoes

THIS DISH IS FRESH AND DELICIOUS, PERFECT FOR A LIGHT LUNCH OR DINNER. IT CAN EVEN BE SERVED AT PARTIES AS APPETIZERS. IT ALL DEPENDS ON HOW RICH THE STUFFING IS AND CONSIDERING THAT IT'S COUSCOUS THAT WE'RE TALKING ABOUT I HAVE TO SAY THAT IT CAN BE AS RICH AS YOU WANT – JUST ADD THE INGREDIENTS YOU FANCY THE MOST.

TIME: 40 MINUTES
SERVES: 10

INGREDIENTS:
1 ½ CUPS COUSCOUS
4 CUPS HOT VEGETABLE STOCK

1 CUP CANNED CHICKPEAS, DRAINED AND CHOPPED
1 CUP CHOPPED PARSLEY
1 CUP CHOPPED CILANTRO
¼ CUP CHOPPED MINT
1 LEMON, JUICED
SALT, PEPPER TO TASTE
½ CUP SLICED ALMONDS
8-10 RIPE TOMATOES

DIRECTIONS:
1. CUT THE TOP OF EACH TOMATO AND SCOOP OUT THE FLESH. SET THE TOMATOES ASIDE.
2. IN A LARGE BOWL, MIX THE COUSCOUS WITH THE HOT STOCK AND LET IT SOAK FOR 20 MINUTES.
3. FLUFF IT UP WITH A FORK AND STIR IN THE REST OF THE INGREDIENTS, EXCEPT THE ALMONDS.
4. ADJUST THE TASTE WITH SALT AND PEPPER THEN SPOON THE COUSCOUS INTO EACH TOMATO.
5. ARRANGE THE TOMATOES ON A PLATTER AND TOP EACH OF THEM WITH SLICED ALMONDS.
6. SERVE THE TOMATOES FRESH.

Basmati Rice with Potato Crust

TIME: 1 ¼ HOURS
SERVES: 6-8

INGREDIENTS:
1 CUP BASMATI RICE
4 CUPS VEGETABLE STOCK
4 TABLESPOONS OLIVE OIL
SALT, PEPPER TO TASTE
1 TEASPOON GARLIC POWDER
3 POTATOES, FINELY SLICED

DIRECTIONS:
1. COMBINE THE RICE WITH 3 CUPS STOCK, OLIVE OIL, SALT AND PEPPER IN A SAUCEPAN AND COOK UNTIL THE LIQUID IS ABSORBED.
2. REMOVE FROM HEAT AND SET ASIDE, STIRRING IN THE REMAINING STOCK.
3. ARRANGE THE POTATOES AT THE BOTTOM OF A PAN THAT CAN GO IN THE OVEN. SPRINKLE THEM WITH GARLIC POWDER THEN SPOON THE RICE OVER THE POTATOES.
4. BAKE IN THE PREHEATED OVEN AT 350F FOR 30 MINUTES.
5. WHEN DONE, REMOVE FROM THE OVEN AND TURN THE RICE UPSIDE DOWN ON A SERVING PLATTER.
6. SERVE THE RICE WARM.

Jeweled Rice

WHAT'S SPECIAL ABOUT THIS RICE IS HOW COLORFUL IT IS AND HOW FLAVORFUL. HAVING SO MANY VEGGIES IN ITS COMPOSITION MAKES IT AN EXCELLENT CHOICE FOR A HEALTHY LUNCH OR DINNER.

TIME: 1 HOUR
SERVES: 4-6

INGREDIENTS:
2 CUPS BASMATI RICE
6 CUPS WATER
1 TEASPOON SALT
¼ CUP OLIVE OIL
1 TEASPOON DEHYDRATED ONION
1 PINCH SAFFRON
1 ORANGE PEEL
1 CUP GREEN PEAS
1 CARROT, DICED
BLACK PEPPER TO TASTE

DIRECTIONS:
1. COMBINE THE RICE WITH THE WATER, SALT AND OLIVE OIL IN A SAUCEPAN AND COOK FOR 30 MINUTES ON LOW HEAT.
2. STIR IN THE REST OF THE INGREDIENTS AND COOK 15-20 MORE MINUTES.
3. SEASON WITH BLACK PEPPER AND SERVE THE RICE WARM.

Stuffed Eggplants

TIME: 1 ¼ HOURS
SERVES: 4

INGREDIENTS:
2 TABLESPOONS OLIVE OIL
1 SHALLOT, CHOPPED
1 GARLIC CLOVE, CHOPPED
1 RIPE TOMATO, DICED
1 CUP COOKED BASMATI RICE
1 CUP CHOPPED PARSLEY
1 TEASPOON DRIED MINT
SALT, PEPPER TO TASTE
2 EGGPLANTS

DIRECTIONS:
1. CUT THE EGGPLANTS IN HALF LENGTHWISE AND SCOOP OUT PART OF THE FLESH. CHOP IT FINELY.
2. HEAT THE OIL IN A SKILLET AND STIR IN THE SHALLOT, GARLIC AND EGGPLANT. SAUTÉ FOR 10 MINUTES, STIRRING OFTEN THEN ADD THE TOMATO, RICE, MINT AND PARSLEY.
3. SEASON WITH SALT AND PEPPER THEN REMOVE FROM HEAT AND SPOON THE MIXTURE BACK INTO THE EGGPLANT SKINS.
4. PLACE THEM ALL ON A BAKING TRAY LINED WITH PARCHMENT PAPER AND BAKE IN THE PREHEATED OVEN AT 350F FOR 40 MINUTES OR UNTIL SOFT.
5. REMOVE FROM THE OVEN AND SERVE THEM RIGHT AWAY.

Desserts
Persian Melon Popsicles

YOU WOULD NEVER THINK ABOUT COMBINING MELON THE WAY THIS RECIPE DOES. BUT ONCE YOU TASTE, YOU GET HOOKED, THAT GOOD AND FRESH IT TASTES. IT IS A GREAT RECIPE FOR SUMMER WHEN MELON IS AT ITS PEAKS.

TIME: 4 HOURS
SERVES: 6-8

INGREDIENTS:
1 MELON, PEELED AND CUBED
2 TABLESPOONS CHOPPED TARRAGON
4 TABLESPOONS AGAVE SYRUP

DIRECTIONS:
1. COMBINE ALL THE INGREDIENTS IN A BLENDER AND PROCESS UNTIL WELL BLENDED.
2. POUR THE MIXTURE IN POPSICLE MOLDS AND FREEZE AT LEAST 3 HOURS.
3. TO REMOVE THE POPSICLES FROM THEIR MOLDS, SINK THEM IN HOT WATER FOR 4-5 SECONDS.
4. SERVE THEM RIGHT AWAY.

Spiced Rice Pudding

TIME: 1 HOUR
SERVES: 4-6

INGREDIENTS:
1 CUP BASMATI RICE
3 CUPS ALMOND OR COCONUT MILK
2 CARDAMOM PODS, CRUSHED
½ CINNAMON STICK
¼ CUP AGAVE SYRUP
1 PINCH SALT
½ CUP SLICED ALMONDS FOR SERVING

DIRECTIONS:
1. RINSE THE RICE WELL AND MIX IT WITH THE MILK IN A HEAVY SAUCEPAN.
2. STIR IN THE AGAVE SYRUP, CARDAMOM AND CINNAMON THEN COOK THE RICE ON LOW HEAT FOR 30-40 MINUTES UNTIL MOST OF THE LIQUID HAS BEEN ABSORBED.
3. ADD A PINCH OF SALT TO BALANCE OUT THE TASTE THEN POUR THE PUDDING IN SERVING BOWLS.
4. TOP WITH SLICED ALMONDS JUST BEFORE SERVING.

Persian Chickpea Flour Cookies

ALTHOUGH THE INGREDIENT LIST IS SLIGHTLY UNUSUAL, THE COOKIES TURN OUT UNEXPECTEDLY TASTY. THEY ARE CRUMBLY AND FLAVORFUL AND THE TASTE IS RATHER EARTHY. THE NUTRITIONAL CONTENT IS HIGH AND THESE COOKIES CAN BECOME GREAT AFTERNOON SNACKS TO CALM YOUR SWEET CRAVINGS.

TIME: 45 MINUTES
YIELDS: 2 DOZEN

INGREDIENTS:
1 CUP COCONUT OIL, SOLID
½ CUP AGAVE SYRUP
2 TABLESPOONS GROUND FLAX SEEDS
1 TEASPOON GROUND CARDAMOM
½ TEASPOON CINNAMON POWDER
2 CUPS CHICKPEA FLOUR
1 PINCH SALT
½ TEASPOON BAKING SODA

DIRECTIONS:
1. COMBINE THE COCONUT OIL WITH THE AGAVE SYRUP IN A BOWL AND MIX WELL.
2. STIR IN THE REST OF THE INGREDIENTS AND MIX VERY WELL.
3. DROP SPOONFULS OF BATTER ON A BAKING TRAY LINED WITH PARCHMENT PAPER AND BAKE THE COOKIES IN THE PREHEATED OVEN AT 350F FOR 20-25 MINUTES.
4. REMOVE FROM THE OVEN WHEN THE EDGES TURN GOLDEN BROWN AND LET THEM COOL DOWN BEFORE SERVING OR STORING IN

AN AIRTIGHT CONTAINER FOR UP TO 1 WEEK.

Persian Halva

HALVA IS AN ORIENTAL DESSERT MADE NOT ONLY IN PERSIA, BUT ALSO IN ISRAEL, IRAQ, IRAN AND TURKEY FOR DECADES NOW. IT'S A SWEET AND FRAGRANT DESSERT THAT TASTES BETTER SERVED CHILLED.

TIME: 1 HOUR
SERVES: 4-6

INGREDIENTS:
1 ½ CUPS ALL-PURPOSE FLOUR
1 CUP AGAVE SYRUP
1 CUP WATER
1 CUP VEGETABLE OIL
1 TEASPOON SAFFRON
1 TEASPOON ROSE WATER

½ CUP PISTACHIO, SHELLED AND CHOPPED
½ CUP SLICED ALMONDS
¼ CUP RAISINS
1 PINCH SALT

DIRECTIONS:
1. HEAT THE OIL IN A SAUCEPAN AND STIR IN THE FLOUR AND SALT. SAUTÉ, STIRRING OFTEN, UNTIL IT BEGINS TO TURN GOLDEN.
2. IN A DIFFERENT SAUCEPAN, COMBINE THE SYRUP WITH 1 CUP WATER AND BRING TO A BOIL. COOK FOR 5 MINUTES THEN ADD THE SAFFRON AND ROSE WATER.
3. POUR THE HOT SYRUP OVER THE FLOUR AND COOK UNTIL IT BEGINS TO THICKEN.
4. STIR IN THE PISTACHIO, RAISINS AND ALMONDS.
5. SPOON THE MIXTURE IN SMALL SERVING BOWLS OR MOLDS AND LET THEM COOL DOWN BEFORE SERVING.
6. IT CAN BE SERVED EITHER SIMPLE OR WITH FRESH FRUITS.

Spiced Carrot Halva

SIMILAR TO THE WHEAT HALVA IN TERMS OF COOKING TECHNIQUE, THIS CARROT HALVA HAS A SPICED, INTENSE TASTE AND IT IS SOMEHOW LIGHTER, THE TASTE IS FRESHER AND THE HALVA ALSO HAS A BEAUTIFUL ORANGE COLOR WHICH MAKES IT FAR MORE APPEALING. I GUESS YOU HAVE TO TRY BOTH RECIPES THEN DECIDE WHICH ONE YOU LIKE MORE.

TIME: 1 HOUR
SERVES: 4-6

INGREDIENTS:
4 CUPS GRATED CARROTS
3 CUPS ALMOND MILK
¾ CUP AGAVE SYRUP
½ CUP VEGETABLE OIL
½ CUP WALNUTS, CHOPPED
½ TEASPOON CARDAMOM POWDER
½ TEASPOON CINNAMON POWDER
1 PINCH NUTMEG

DIRECTIONS:
1. COMBINE THE MILK WITH THE AGAVE SYRUP AND BRING TO A BOIL.
2. HEAT THE OIL IN A HEAVY SAUCEPAN AND STIR IN THE CARROTS. SAUTÉ FOR 10 MINUTES THEN POUR IN THE SYRUP AND KEEP COOKING FOR 20-30 MINUTES UNTIL THE MIXTURE BEGINS TO THICKEN.
3. REMOVE FROM HEAT AND STIR IN THE WALNUTS AND SPICES.
4. SPOON THE HALVA IN INDIVIDUAL SERVING BOWLS AND LET IT COOL DOWN COMPLETELY

BEFORE SERVING.

Cinnamon Date Cake

TIME: 1 HOUR
SERVES: 6-8

INGREDIENTS:
3 CUPS PITTED DATES
1 CUP WALNUTS, CHOPPED
1 CUP COCONUT OIL, MELTED
1 ½ CUPS ALL-PURPOSE FLOUR
½ CUP AGAVE SYRUP
1 TEASPOON CINNAMON POWDER
½ TEASPOON GROUND CARDAMOM
1 PINCH SALT
1 TEASPOON BAKING SODA
1 CUP COCONUT, SHREDDED
1 CUP PISTACHIO, CHOPPED

DIRECTIONS:
1. COMBINE THE DATES WITH THE WALNUTS, COCONUT OIL AND AGAVE SYRUP IN A FOOD PROCESSOR OR BLENDER AND PULSE UNTIL SMOOTH.
2. STIR IN THE FLOUR, SPICES, SALT AND BAKING POWDER THEN FOLD IN THE SHREDDED COCONUT AND PISTACHIO.
3. SPOON THE BATTER IN A ROUND CAKE PAN LINED WITH PARCHMENT PAPER.
4. BAKE THE CAKE IN THE PREHEATED OVEN AT 350F FOR 30-40 MINUTES.
5. TO CHECK IF THE CAKE IS DONE, INSERT A TOOTHPICK IN THE CENTER OF THE CAKE. IF IT COMES OUT CLEAN, THE CAKE IS DONE BUT IF IT STILL HAS TRACES OF BATTER, BAKE THE CAKE A FEW MORE MINUTES THEN CHECK AGAIN.

6. WHEN DONE, REMOVE FROM THE OVEN AND LET IT COOL DOWN BEFORE SLICING AND SERVING.

Wild Rice Apricot Pudding

TIME: 50 MINUTES
SERVES: 4-6

INGREDIENTS:
1 CUP WILD RICE
3 CUPS ALMOND MILK
2 TABLESPOONS CORNSTARCH
½ CUP AGAVE SYRUP
½ TEASPOON VANILLA EXTRACT
½ CUP SLICED ALMONDS FOR SERVING
½ CUP APRICOT JAM

DIRECTIONS:
1. COMBINE THE RICE WITH THE MILK IN A HEAVY SAUCEPAN AND BRING TO A BOIL. LOWER THE HEAT AND COOK THE RICE FOR 20-30 MINUTES UNTIL MOST OF THE LIQUID HAS BEEN ABSORBED.
2. STIR IN THE CORNSTARCH AND AGAVE SYRUP AND COOK A FEW MORE MINUTES UNTIL IT THICKENS.
3. REMOVE FROM HEAT AND STIR IN THE VANILLA. SPOON THE PUDDING IN INDIVIDUAL SERVING BOWLS AND LET THEM COOL DOWN BEFORE SERVING.
4. TOP WITH APRICOT JAM AND SLICED ALMONDS JUST BEFORE SERVING IT.

Melon and Cherry Compote

COMPOTE IS AMAZING DURING SUMMER, ESPECIALLY SERVED CHILLED. IT IS A VERSATILE RECIPE AND YOU CAN APPLY THIS COOKING TECHNIQUE TO MANY OTHER FRUITS, FROM PEACHES TO APRICOTS, SOUR CHERRIES OR GRAPES.

TIME: 30 MINUTES
SERVES: 2-4

INGREDIENTS:
2 CUPS MELON CUBES
2 CUPS CHERRIES
1 CUP WATER
1 CUP ORANGE JUICE
2 TABLESPOONS AGAVE SYRUP
½ CINNAMON STICK
1 STAR ANISE
1 LEMON SLICE

DIRECTIONS:
1. COMBINE THE MELON WITH THE CHERRIES, WATER AND ORANGE JUICE IN A SAUCEPAN.
2. STIR IN THE AGAVE SYRUP, CINNAMON STICK, LEMON SLICE AND STAR ANISE AND BRING TO BOIL.
3. COOK THE COMPOTE FOR 20 MINUTES ON LOW HEAT, MAKING SURE THE FRUITS ARE TENDER BUT NOT MUSHY.
4. REMOVE FROM HEAT AND DISCARD THE CINNAMON STICK, LEMON SLICE AND STAR ANISE.
5. LET IT COOL DOWN THEN SERVE CHILLED.

Persian Sweet Rice

TIME: 1 HOUR
SERVES: 4-6

INGREDIENTS:
1 ½ CUPS BASMATI RICE, RINSED
¼ CUP COCONUT OIL
½ CUP AGAVE SYRUP
2 CUPS GRATED CARROTS
½ CUP SLICED ALMONDS
½ CUP CHOPPED DATES
½ CUP CHOPPED DRIED FIGS
¼ CUP PUMPKIN SEEDS
1 TEASPOON GROUND CARDAMOM
½ TEASPOON CINNAMON POWDER
1 TEASPOON TURMERIC

DIRECTIONS:
1. STEAM THE RICE UNTIL SOFT AND FLUFFED UP. REMOVE FROM HEAT AND FLUFF IT UP WITH A FORK THEN SET ASIDE.
2. HEAT THE OIL IN A SKILLET AND STIR IN THE CARROTS. SAUTÉ FOR 10 MINUTES THEN ADD THE REST OF THE INGREDIENTS.
3. COOK FOR 10 MORE MINUTES THEN STIR IN THE RICE.
4. SAUTÉ FOR 15 MINUTES, STIRRING OFTEN THEN REMOVE FROM HEAT AND SERVE THE RICE WARM OR CHILLED.

Ranginak – Date and Walnut Squares

TIME: 1 HOUR
SERVES: 4-6

INGREDIENTS:
2 CUPS ALL-PURPOSE FLOUR
2 CUPS PITTED DATES
½ CUP AGAVE SYRUP
1 CUP WALNUTS, GROUND
1 TEASPOON CINNAMON POWDER
½ TEASPOON CARDAMOM POWDER
1 CUP VEGETABLE OIL
1 PINCH SALT

DIRECTIONS:
1. HEAT THE OIL IN A HEAVY SAUCEPAN AND STIR IN THE FLOUR. COOK FOR 15-20 MINUTES, STIRRING OFTEN, UNTIL THE FLOUR TURNS GOLDEN BROWN. STIR IN THE AGAVE SYRUP AND WALNUTS, AS WELL AS THE SPICES AND A PINCH OF SALT.
2. REMOVE FROM HEAT AND SPREAD HALF OF THE MIXTURE IN A SQUARE PAN.
3. TOP WITH PITTED DATES THEN COVER WITH THE REMAINING FLOUR MIXTURE.
4. REFRIGERATE 1 HOUR THEN CUT IN SMALL SQUARES AND SERVE.

Conclusion

THE PERSIAN CUISINE IS AN EXPLOSION OF COLOR AND FLAVOR, A CUISINE THAT IMPRESSES WITH EVERY ASPECT, FROM BALANCED SPICES TO BOLD FLAVORS AND UNUSUAL COMBINATIONS. BUT APART FROM THIS, IT IS A CUISINE BASED ON FRESH FRUITS AND VEGGIES MORE THAN ON ANYTHING ELSE AND THAT MAKES THE TRANSITION FROM A COMMON DIET TO A VEGAN ONE MUCH EASIER. SALADS, SOUPS, STEWS OR STUFFED VEGGIES ARE ALL EASY TO COOK AND OFFER AMAZING EATING EXPERIENCES FOR THE ENTIRE FAMILY.

ALL YOU HAVE TO DO IS PUT THAT APRON ON AND GET ADVENTUROUS IN THE KITCHEN! YOU HAVE NO IDEA HOW MUCH SATISFACTION COOKING SOMETHING FROM SCRATCH OFFERS YOU, ESPECIALLY WHEN WE ARE TALKING ABOUT SUCH FRAGRANT AND SPECIAL DISHES.

Healthy Vegan Moroccan recipes

By Bryan Rylee

Healthy Vegan Moroccan recipeS
Copyright ©2014 by Bryan Rylee.
All rights reserved. No part of this book
May be used or reproduced in any matter
Whatsoever without permission in writing from
The author except in the case of brief quotations
Embodied in critical articles or review.

Disclaimer:

The information presented in this book represents the views of the publisher as of the date of publication. The publisher reserves the rights to alter update their opinions based on new conditions. This report is for informational purposes only. The author and the publisher do not accept any responsibilities for any liabilities resulting from the use of this information. While every attempt has been made to verify the information provided here, the author and the publisher cannot assume any responsibility for errors, inaccuracies or omissions. Any similarities with people or facts are unintentional.

Table of Contents

Introduction 5

- The Moroccan Vegan Cuisine – Most Common Ingredients 9
- Appetizers 12
- Moroccan Chickpea Patties 12
- Moroccan Roasted Vegetables 18
- Moroccan Pumpkin Hummus 20
- Grilled Eggplants in honey and Harissa 22
- Moroccan-Spiced Carrot-Date Salad 28
- Moroccan Couscous Salad 31
- Soups and stews 37
- Moroccan Carrot Red Lentil Soup 37
- Chickpea and Winter Vegetable Stew 41
- Moroccan Red Gazpacho 43
- Moroccan Harira (Bean Soup) 47
- Main Dishes 51
- Sweet and Nutty Moroccan Couscous 51
- Sweet Potato, Chickpea and Zucchini Tagine 55
- Vegan Moroccan Stuffed Squash 57
- Vegan Moroccan Tagine 59
- Couscous Shepherd's Pie 62
- Desserts 68
- Oranges with Caramel and Cardamom Syrup 68
- Moroccan Apple Dessert 72
- Moroccan Charoset Balls 73
- Moroccan Sesame Seed cookies 77
- Honey Almond Stuffed Dates 80

Introduction

Thank you for choosing this cookbook, "Healthy Vegan Moroccan Recipes".
I hope it will be able to guide you through the process of enjoying healthy traditional meals, making your time in the kitchen pleasant. Recipes included in this cookbook provide you an easy way to get acquainted with Moroccan cooking culture and cook healthy and at the same time delicious vegan food, including soups, stews made of vegetables, legumes, greens, salads, as well as desserts.
Many may argue that there is no Moroccan vegan cuisine but I assure you that there is a rich variety of vegetarian meals from several cuisines you can see in that region. These tendencies influenced the way and content of what Moroccans eat. You can even see the history of the country through its food. Being a country located on the shore of the Northern Africa, it incorporates Mediterranean and Northern African traditional cuisines. But the influence on the Moroccan cuisine was not limited with the above mentioned cuisines. In Morocco you can see and feel the presence of not only Persian flavor of such stuff like saffron, nuts, pickled lemon and pomegranates but also Spanish culinary like olive, olive oil, pepper and salt which were introduced in Morocco in the Middle ages. So taking into account the richness and available diversity in Moroccan meals, we can claim certainly that the Moroccan cuisine and particularly vegetarian is one of the most balanced cuisines in the world with strong focus on flavors and aromas, wide range of spices and fresh ingredients making the Moroccan food very delicious and tasty indeed.
It's worth mentioning the hospitality of Moroccan people. In Morocco, guests are offered tea and food within seconds upon entering home. Moroccan mint tea, or as Moroccans jokingly call it, the"Moroccan whiskey", is widely consumed all across Morocco.
Moroccan People drink tea all day between meals.
The main course which you will often meet in the Moroccan cuisine is couscous prepared of fine semolina grains. In Morocco, couscous is always steamed, until it is pale and fluffy. It is generally served with stewed or sautéed spicy vegetables (carrots, potatoes, turnips, *etc.*) or with some meat chicken, beef or lamb. In Morocco, couscous can be

served just by itself as a main dish or as a sweet delicacy, sprinkled with raisin, toasted ground almonds, sugar and cinnamon.

The other famous dish is tagine that is traditionally cooked in clay pots known by the same name. The tagine is a rich tasty stew made of vegetables, legumes, fruit and lots of spices. In vegan versions only various vegetables, legumes fruit and nuts are added to the stew. Every part of the country has its own variety of tagine and various ways of preparing it. As it takes long to cook this meal, housewives start preparing the lunch tagine as soon as breakfast is over.

Bread (*Khobz*) is also an essential part of the Moroccan cuisine. Moroccan bread is a round and flat loaf with lots of pleasant golden crust. In some families it is baked in wood burning ovens which provide it with a unique taste. People sometimes add anise and cumin to the bread for extra flavor.

Vegetables are also an important part of Moroccan food. Carrot, potato, zucchini, onion, and pumpkin are the most common vegetables in Moroccan cooking. They are used raw, pickled or cooked in salads, soups, tagines and other dishes. Specifically, eggplant can be found in many fried dishes and many cooked vegetable salads.

As for fruits, Moroccan people eat fruit for dessert. They eat either fresh or dried fruits, such as apricot, grape, apple, plum, orange, fig, date, and peach. Fruits are often used to prepare healthy vegan desserts flavored with sweet spicy syrups.

One cannot imagine Moroccan cuisine without herbs and spices. They are used in various types, fresh or dried, whole or ground. Cilantro and parsley are the most widely used herbs in cooking and they are added to almost all dishes providing them with fresh and pleasant taste and look. The most popular among the spices are saffron, cumin, paprika, turmeric, and cinnamon, onion. Moroccan cuisine is well known for its spice mixtures. The most common among them are Harissa and Ras el Hanout. Harissa is a hot chilli paste made of various peppers, herbs and spices, such as coriander seeds, garlic paste and some olive oil or vegetable oil for preservation. Ras el Hanout is a spice blend that can be made of about 30 ground spices, but the key spices included are cinnamon, cardamom, nutmeg, anise, ginger, turmeric, various peppers, and mace.

8

The Moroccan Vegan Cuisine – Most Common Ingredients

Chickpeas or garbanzo beans are an important part of Moroccan cuisine. Chickpeas are rich in fiber and proteins. Beans are also perfect food for people trying to lose weight, as eating small portions keeps you full for a long time. Along with other legumes, such as lentils, split peas, beans, chickpeas are used in salads, soups, stews and tagines.

Green herbs -there are a lot of herbs used in Moroccan cuisine that provide distinct and unique flavors to any dish. But Cilantro and parsley are the most widely used herbs in Moroccan cooking and essential ingredients in fresh salads, soups, stews, etc. The other most essential herb is used to prepare the favorite Moroccan mint tea. Apart from their distinctive and fresh taste, green herbs are also a good source of vitamins and antioxidants.

Oils – olive oil is arguably the best oil to make the healthiest Moroccan dishes. They use it in seasoning salads, cooking soups, and in baking. It can also be served in a small dish or a bottle as a condiment with bread, or as a garnish for cooked salads. As the olive oil is sometimes considered very expensive for the average Moroccan, many households use vegetable oil in their cooking.

Dried Fruits and Nuts - you can find dates in many Moroccan recipes. Morocco's most commonly consumed dates are Medjoul dates; It is a sweet date with a velvety texture. They are commonly used in tagines and in making various sweet delicacies. Apart from dates, other dried fruits, such as dried apricots and raisins are used in Moroccan cooking. Walnuts and Almonds are the most commonly used nuts in the Moroccan cuisine. They are used both, as a key ingredient or as a garnish. Almonds alongside dried apricots are mostly used in making tagines as well as in preparing Moroccan amazing desserts and sweets. Nuts are a great source of fibers and healthy fats and have a rich flavor providing nice crunch to any dish.

Lemons - Lemon is another prevailing ingredient in many recipes. Both its juice and rind are edible in Moroccan culinary. Lemon juice is commonly used in preparing dressings for fresh salads. They provide a pungent citrus aroma to the sweets and desserts of Moroccan cuisine.

Saffron - is known to be the most expensive spice in the world. It is used in culinary not only for its unique taste, but also for its coloring properties. Saffron provides a nice orange color to any food that includes saffron in the ingredient list. In the Moroccan cuisine you will find saffron almost in every dish, in stews, soups, salads, and sometimes even in desserts. Store saffron in an airtight container in a dark and cool place to longer preserve its bright color and aromatic features.

Turmeric- is a bright yellow powder made from turmeric rhizomes. Turmeric has a warm and bitter taste and is used extensively as a food flavoring and dye. In Morocco, it is mainly used to make curry powders and other seasoning blends. Turmeric has a high nutritional profile. It has a good source of vitamins and minerals that are known to have antioxidant properties.

Cumin It is widely used in Moroccan cooking to season salads, beans, soups, some tagines and stews, grilled and roasted meats and more. In Morocco, *Cumin* is considered to be so essential that it is served with meal along with salt and pepper. As long as it has a strong and distinctive flavor, use it in moderate amounts when seasoning the dish. Cumin is a good source of vitamins and minerals that are known to have antioxidant properties.

Appetizers

Moroccan Chickpea Patties

These Moroccan spicy chickpea patties will melt in your mouth. Make sure you have all the ingredients at hand and get ready for this special treat.
Prep time 6 minutes
Cook time: 15 minutes
Serves 8

Ingredients:
1 small onion, diced
2-3 cloves garlic, peeled
1 tablespoon olive or vegetable oil plus a bit for frying
1 can chickpeas rinsed and drained (or 1-1.5 cups cooked)
1 lemon, juiced
1/4 cup chickpea or oat flour + 2 tablespoons for coating
2 tablespoons parsley
1 teaspoon cumin
1/4 teaspoon cinnamon
1 teaspoon salt
1/2 teaspoon ground coriander
1/4 teaspoon cayenne
1/4 teaspoon black pepper
1/4 teaspoon ground ginger

Directions:
1. Heat the olive oil in a medium frying pan over medium-high heat.
2. Add the garlic and onion and sauté until the onions are golden and translucent, about 4 minutes.
3. Add the chickpeas to a microwave safe bowl and heat 2 minutes on High, until heated through.
4. Place the warm chickpeas, cooked onions, chickpea flour, garlic, parsley lemon juice, cinnamon, cumin, cayenne, coriander, ginger and black pepper in a blender.
5. Pulse until the mixture resembles smooth thick paste.
6. Using your hands shape patties and coat them with flour.
7. Add a few tablespoons of oil to a large nonstick skillet and set over a medium heat.
8. Once it starts sizzling, place the patties in the hot oil and fry for about 3 minutes per side until patties acquire golden crust.
9. Serve the burgers with fresh veggie salad or on a bun.

Moroccan Carrot Dip

Carrots are very popular in Moroccan cuisine, and it is valued for the health benefits, that it provides. In this dish, a new preparation method is suggested. Make sure not to brown carrots when cooking to get a nice orange color.

Prep time: 40 minutes
Cook time: 25 minutes
Serves: 2-4 servings

Ingredients:
3 tablespoons extra-virgin olive oil
2 lbs carrots (about 12), peeled and sliced
2 garlic cloves, minced
3/4 teaspoon ground coriander
3/4 teaspoon ground cumin
3/4 teaspoon ground ginger
1/8 teaspoon chili powder
1/8 teaspoon ground cinnamon
1/3 cup water
1 tablespoon white wine vinegar
1 tablespoon minced fresh cilantro
Salt
Pepper

Directions:

1. Add 1 tablespoon of the olive oil to a large griddle and set over medium-high heat.
2. Once sizzling, add the carrots and 1/2 teaspoon salt and cook until crisp-tender, 4-6 minutes.
3. Stir in the cumin, garlic, cinnamon coriander, chili powder and ginger and sauté until fragrant, about half a minute. Add the water and bring to a boil.

4. Then slow down the heat to low, and let simmer, covered, stirring often, until the carrots are tender, 18- 20 minutes.
5. Remove the griddle from the heat and using a potato masher, mash the carrots.
6. Add the vinegar and remaining 2 tablespoons oil. Transfer to a bowl and chill in the refrigerator for 25 minutes, covered.
7. Season them with salt and pepper to taste, garnish with chopped cilantro and enjoy.
8. The dip can be refrigerated in an airtight container for up to 2 days. Season with additional vinegar, salt and pepper to taste and sprinkle with the cilantro before serving.

Moroccan Roasted Vegetables

These roasted vegetables flavored with Moroccan spices are an easy side for vegan dinner party. Try to cut the red pepper into thin strips as they provide a pleasant lookto this dish.

Prep Time: 20 minutes
Cook Time: 40 minutes
Serves 6

1 medium onion cut in slices
1 medium zucchini cut in half moons
1 small eggplant, peeled, cut into half moons
1 large sweet potato, peeled, cut into half moons
1 large red pepper, sliced in 1/4-inch strips
2 medium tomatoes, fresh, chopped
15 oz. (420 g) chickpeas, drained and rinsed
3 garlic cloves, minced
2 tablespoons olive oil
1 tablespoon lemon juice

1 tablespoon cumin
1 1/2 teaspoons turmeric
1 1/2 teaspoons cinnamon
1 1/2 teaspoons paprika
1/4 teaspoon cayenne

Directions:
1. Place the zucchini, eggplant, onion, potato, red pepper, tomatoes, chickpeas and garlic in a large salad bowl.
2. In a small bowl, mix together the lemon juice, cumin, turmeric, cinnamon, paprika, cayenne and olive oil.
3. Pour the mixture over the vegetables and toss to combine.
4. Place the vegetables in a rimmed baking dish and bake in the oven for about 35-40 minutes, stirring 2-3 times.

Moroccan Pumpkin Hummus

Prep time: 10 minutes
Cook time: 5 minutes
Serves 4-6

Hummus is arguably the healthiest dip that you can feel free to indulge in. It is delicious with grilled pita bread, carrots or even simply whole wheat crackers. And tahini is typically what makes hummus taste like hummus.

Ingredients:
1 tablespoon olive oil
2 garlic cloves, chopped
1 teaspoon ground ginger
1 teaspoon ground coriander
1/4 teaspoon cinnamon
1/4 teaspoon ground allspice
1/4 teaspoon turmeric
1/8 teaspoon cayenne
1/4 teaspoon sugar
2 tablespoons tahini
1 cup home-cooked or canned chickpeas
1 cup canned solid-pack pumpkin (or fresh cooked winter squash or pumpkin!)
2 tablespoons fresh lemon juice
1/2 teaspoon salt
1/4 teaspoon black pepper
1 tablespoon pistachios, chopped for garnish

Directions:
1. Add 1 tablespoon olive to a frying pan and set over medium heat.
2. Add the ginger, garlic, cinnamon, coriander, turmeric, allspice, cayenne, and sugar and sauté for 1-2 minutes.
3. Add the chickpeas and tahini, give a stir and then remove the pan from the heat.
4. Add the lemon juice, pumpkin, season with salt and pepper. Let cool.
5. Add the mixture to a food processor and pulse until smooth.
6. Place the hummus into a serving bowl, sprinkle with the chopped pistachios and serve.
7. Great to chill for a couple of hours before serving.

8.

Grilled Eggplants in honey and Harissa

The amazing flavors of eggplant and honey are paired with harissa in this satisfying tasty dish. Enjoy with freshly cooked rice.

Prep time: 5 minutes
Cook time: 18 minutes
Serves 4
Ingredients:
2 eggplants, peeled and thickly sliced
Olive oil for frying
2-3 garlic cloves, crushed
2- inch piece of fresh root ginger, peeled and grated
1 teaspoon ground cumin
1 teaspoon harissa
3 tablespoons honey
Juice of 1 lemon
Sea salt

Directions:

1. Preheat the grill to medium. Coat the eggplant slices with olive oil and grill on both sides, until lightly golden.
2. Heat little olive oil in a large skillet over medium heat. Add the garlic and sauté for 30 seconds.
3. Add the cumin, ginger, honey, lemon juice and harissa and stir fry for a few seconds.
4. Add enough water so that it covers the base of the skillet, and arrange the eggplant slices in the skillet. Let cook until all liquid is absorbed, about 10 minutes. Add little extra water if needed. Season with salt and let cool.
5. Serve the dish with fresh bread. .

Moroccan Mashed Potatoes

If you are fond of potato, then this Moroccan dish would serve your appetite ideally. The addition of spices gave it an unforgettable taste.

Prep time: 20 minutes
Cook time: 15 minutes
Serves 32

Ingredients:
10 largebaking potatoes, peeled and cubed
3 tablespoonsolive oil, or as needed
1onion, diced
1 tablespoonground turmeric
1 tablespoonsalt, or to taste
2 teaspoonsground black pepper
1/2 teaspoonground cumin

Directions:
1. Put the potatoes into a large saucepan; pour in enough water to cover and bring to a boil over medium-high heat.
2. Cook for about 23-25 minute, until potatoes are soft.
3. Add 1 tablespoon olive oil to a frying pan and set over medium-high heat.
4. Add the onion and sauté until golden and translucent, about 5minutes.
5. Pour off the potato cooking liquid and mash the potatoes, add the cooked onion, cumin, turmeric, season with salt and pepper and continue mashing.
6. Add the remaining 2 tablespoons of olive oil and stir well to make creamy puree.

Salads
Moroccan Carrot-Chickpea Salad

This is a fantastic salad and can be served with any main course. It goes well with greens and rice. It is very tasty and aromatic, let alone the benefits of carrots, raisins and cashews.

Prep time: 20 minutes
Cook time: 0 minutes
Serves 8
Ingredients:
Zest and juice of 1 lemon
1 teaspoon ground coriander
1/8 teaspoon cayenne pepper
1 ¼ teaspoon salt
1/3 cup Extra Virgin Olive oil
1 ½ lbs (700 g) carrots, coarsely grated
2 cans (15 oz.) chickpeas, rinsed
1/2 cup golden raisins
1/2 cup roasted, unsalted cashews, coarsely chopped
1/3 cup coarsely chopped cilantro, plus leaves for garnish
1/3 cup fresh mint, chopped

Directions;
1. In a large salad bowl, whisk together the olive oil, lemon zest and juice, cayenne, coriander and 1 1/4 teaspoon of salt.
2. Add the chickpeas, carrots, cashews, raisins, mint and chopped cilantro and mix to combine. Let stand for at least 10 minutes. Garnish the salad with cilantro leaves and serve.

Moroccan Lentil Salad

The combination of garbanzo beans, tomatoes and colorful peppers flavored with lemon juice makes this salad delicious and a first choice of people looking for a healthy food.

Prep time: 40 minutes
Cook time: 40minutes
Serves 5
Ingredients:
1/2 cup dry lentils
1 1/2 cups water
1/2 (15 ounce) can garbanzo beans, drained
2 tomatoes, chopped
4 green onions, chopped
2 hot green chili peppers, minced
1 green bell pepper, chopped
1/2 yellow bell pepper, chopped
1 red bell pepper, chopped
1 lime, juiced
2 tablespoons olive oil
1/4 cup fresh cilantro, chopped
Salt to taste

Directions:

1. Add lentils to a medium saucepan, pour in the water and set over medium-high heat.

2. Once boiling, slow down the heat and let simmer, until soft, about 30 minutes.

3. Place the cooked lentils, green onions, tomatoes, chickpeas, bell peppers, green chilies in a medium salad bowl, add the olive oil, lime juice and chopped cilantro.

4. Season the salad with salt to taste and mix well to combine.

5. Refrigerate for 30 minutes before serving.

Moroccan-Spiced Carrot-Date Salad

This is a wonderful salad full of refreshing flavors. Make sure you have all the ingredients on hand and start experiencing.

Prep Time: 45 minutes
Cook Time: 5 minutes
Serves: 6

Ingredients:
Salad:
1 lb (450 g) carrots, grated
1 oz. (30 g) fresh flat leaf parsley, coarsely chopped (about ½ cup chopped)
1 medium white onion, halved and thinly sliced
4 medium Medjool dates, pitted, halved, and thinly sliced cross-wise
2 medium navel oranges, peeled and sliced cross-wise
Dressing:
3 tablespoons fresh lemon juice
3 tablespoons olive oil
2 medium cloves garlic, crushed
½ teaspoon salt
½ teaspoon ground sweet paprika
¼ teaspoon ground coriander
¼ teaspoon ground black pepper
⅛ teaspoon ground cinnamon

Directions:
1. Using a mandolin, thinly slice the carrots into ribbons and transfer to a large bowl of ice water. Let them stand for 20-25 minutes, until curled
2. Remove from the water and drain. Place the carrots in a large bowl, add the oranges, dates, onion and chopped parsley.
3. In a small bowl, mix together the olive oil, lemon juice, garlic, paprika, coriander, cinnamon,
4. Pour the dressing over the salad and mix to combine.
5. Enjoy.

Moroccan Couscous Salad

This is a very simple, but very tasty Moroccan dish. The mandarin oranges, chickpeas and bell peppers provide it a wonderful flavor and look.

Prep Time: 15 minutes
Cook Time: 5 minutes
Servings: 6-8

Ingredients:
1/4cup peanut oil or 1/4cupolive oil
1/4teaspoonturmeric
1/4teaspooncinnamon
1/4teaspoonground ginger
1/4teaspooncumin
1/4teaspooncayenne
1 1/2-2 cupscouscous
2 1/2cupswater or 2 1/2cupsvegetable stock

1/4 cup orange juice
1-2 tablespoon brown sugar
1 (15 oz. /420 g) can chickpeas
1 (8 oz./230 g) can mandarin oranges
1 red onion, chopped
1 green bell peppers or 1 red bell pepper, chopped
1/4 cup golden raisin
2-3 tablespoons fresh cilantro
2 tablespoons peanuts (optional) or 2 tablespoons almonds (optional)
Salt

Directions:
1. Add 1 tablespoon of oil to a medium pot and set over medium-high heat. Add the turmeric, cumin, cayenne, ginger, cinnamon and uncooked couscous and stir fry until fragrant, about 1-2 minutes.
2. Pour in the vegetable stock and bring to a boil.
3. Slow down the heat, put the lid on and let simmer until all liquid is absorbed, about 5 minutes. Turn off the heat and let stand about 5 minutes.
4. Using a fork, gently fluff the couscous and transfer it to a medium salad bowl. Add the onion, bell peppers, chickpeas, mandarin oranges and raisins.
5. Make the dressing by combining orange juice, sugar and 3 tablespoons oil in a small bowl. Season the dressing with salt and pour over the salad. Mix well to combine,
6. Sprinkle the salad with nuts and cilantro. Chill for about 30 minutes and enjoy.

Moroccan Carrot Quinoa Salad with Tahini Dressing

Sweet from maple syrup, sour from lemon and flavored with lots of spices, this humble salad manages to get all taste buds firing at once.

Prep Time: 45 minutes
Cook Time: 5 minutes
Serves: 4

Ingredients:
4 carrots
5 oz. (150 g) cooked chickpeas
1/4 cup uncooked quinoa
5 oz. (150 g) potatoes (about 3-4 small)
6 1/3 oz. (180 g) cauliflower
1 ½ oz. (40 g) dried figs
1 teaspoon pine nuts
1 teaspoon olive oil
1 teaspoon cumin
1/8 teaspoon sweet smoked paprika
a pinch of spicy paprika
For the dressing
1 teaspoon extra virgin olive oil
1 teaspoon tahini
1 teaspoon maple syrup (or honey)
1 teaspoon lemon juice
Handful of parsley

Directions:
1. Cook the potatoes in a medium pot until soft.
2. Cook the quinoa following the package instructions.
3. Add 1 teaspoon of olive oil to a large frying pan and heat over medium heat. Add the chopped potatoes, chickpeas, cauliflower, and cooked quinoas, season with paprika, cumin and salt and pepper to taste.
4. Using a mandolin or a vegetable peeler, thinly slice the carrots into ribbons.
5. Cut figs into smaller pieces.
6. Place all salad ingredients in a bowl and pour the dressing over the salad.

Zaalouk

Very tasty and traditional Moroccan salad. Add some freshly squeezed lemon juice to the salad to make the taste complete.
Prep time: 10 minutes
Cook time: 50 minutes
Serves 4

Ingredients:
2 large eggplants
3 large tomatoes
2-3 garlic cloves peeled and chopped
½ cup good olive oil
1 tablespoon of fresh coriander chopped
1/2 tsp sweet paprika
Juice of 1 lemon (or to taste)
Ground cumin to serve
Salt

Directions:
1. Preheat the oven to 400 F (200 C).
2. Place the eggplants on a baking sheet and bake in the oven until tender, about 25 minutes.
3. Place the tomatoes in a roasting tin, with 1/4 cup of the olive oil and roast for 5-10 minutes.
4. Withdraw the eggplants and tomatoes from the oven and let cool. Halve the baked eggplants, scoop out the pulp with a spoon and chop.
5. Remove the skin and seeds from tomatoes, and chop the pulp. Skin the tomatoes and remove the seed and chop the flesh also to a pulp.
6. Add the remaining oil to a medium skillet and set over moderate heat. Add the garlic and sauté for a few seconds.
7. Add the eggplants, tomatoes and paprika and cook for 8-10 minutes, stirring frequently. In the end, add the coriander, salt and lemon juice, gently stir to combine.
8. Place the salad in a serving bowl, sprinkle with cumin and serve with fresh bread.
9. Great to enjoy warm or at room temperature.

Soups and stews

Moroccan Carrot Red Lentil Soup

Prep time 10 minutes
Cook time 35 minutes
Serves: 8

Easy and tasty soup full of healthy vegetables and spices. This dish is perfect especially for cold winter.

Ingredients:
2 tablespoons olive oil

1 sweet onion, chopped
3 garlic cloves, minced
7 carrots, peeled, chopped
1 teaspoon cumin
1 teaspoon turmeric
2 teaspoon coriander
½ teaspoon paprika
¼ teaspoon cinnamon
2 cups red lentils, rinsed until water runs clear
1-15 oz can diced tomatoes
6 cups vegetable broth
Salt and pepper, to taste
Fresh cilantro, fresh lemon juice and crushed red pepper, to garnish

Directions:
1. Add 2 tablespoons of olive oil to a large saucepan and place over medium heat.
2. Add the garlic and onion and sauté until tender.
3. Stir in the carrots and sauté until carrots have softened, about 10 minutes.
4. Add the cinnamon, cumin, coriander, paprika, turmeric and cook for another 2 minutes.
5. Add the diced tomatoes, lentils and vegetable broth, give a stir to combine and let simmer over low heat until lentils are soft, for about 35 minutes.
6. To make a creamy soup, blend it in portions or you may use an immersion blender.
7. Ladle the soup into serving bowls, sprinkle with fresh cilantro and red pepper.
8. Serve with fresh lemon juice.

Roasted Tomato Soup with Olive Toasts

This delicious soup is full of great flavors. It looks nice and tastes great.

Prep time 20 minutes
Cook time: 1 hr 30 minutes
Serves 8
Ingredients:
2 1/4 lbs (1100 g) plum tomatoes cut in half lengthwise
2 garlic cloves, unpeeled
2 medium sweet onions, thinly sliced
1/2 red bell pepper, seeded
Cooking spray
1 1/2 teaspoons olive oil
1/2 teaspoon ground cumin
1/2 teaspoon ground coriander
1 teaspoon harissa
1/4 teaspoon Spanish smoked paprika
2 1/2 cups vegetable broth
1/2 cup water
1/2 teaspoon fresh thyme, chopped
1 1/2 teaspoons fresh lemon juice
1/8 teaspoon salt
1/8 teaspoon freshly ground black pepper
Toasts:
1 garlic clove, halved
8 (1/4-inch-thick) slices of French bread baguette, toasted
1/4 cup pitted Kalamata olives, chopped
1 1/2 teaspoons chopped fresh parsley
1/4 teaspoon balsamic vinegar
1/8 teaspoon fresh thyme, chopped

Directions:
1. Preheat oven to 425°F (220 °C).
2. Coat a baking sheet with cooking spray. Place the halved tomatoes, cut sides up, 2 garlic onion slices, cloves, and bell pepper half on the prepared baking sheet and bake in the oven until brown, about 60-70 minutes. Remove from the oven and let cool.
3. Cut the onion, tomatoes, and bell pepper. Reserve 1/3 cup chopped onion for the toasts. Squeeze the baked garlic cloves to extract pulp and discard the skins.
4. Add the olive oil to a griddle and set over medium heat.
5. Stir in the bell pepper, remaining chopped onion, cumin and coriander; sauté for 5 minutes, stirring often.
6. Stir in the paprika and harissa, cook for another 2-3 minutes.
7. Add the garlic pulp, tomatoes, water, broth, and 1/2 teaspoon thyme; bring to a boil.
8. Slow down the heat and let simmer, covered, 12-15 minutes.
9. Add the lemon juice, season with salt and black pepper and let stand 5 minutes.
10. Blend the tomato soup in a food processor in 2 batches until smooth.
11. Make the toasts. Rub one side of each baguette slice with halved garlic clove.
12. In a small bowl, mix together the olives, vinegar, 1/8 teaspoon thyme, parsley and reserved 1/3 cup chopped onion. Place about 1 tablespoon olive mixture onto each bread slice and spread evenly.
13. Ladle the soup into serving bowls and serve with an olive toast.

Chickpea and Winter Vegetable Stew

A nice combination of vegetables and spices. And it is also rich in proteins and vitamins. This stew is very filling and perfect for lunch or dinner.

Prep time 15 minutes
Cook time 40 minutes
Serves 8

6. **Ingredients:**

2 teaspoons extra-virgin olive oil
1 cup chopped onion
1 cup (1/2-inch) slices leek
1/2 teaspoon ground coriander
1/2 teaspoon caraway seeds, crushed
1/8 teaspoon cumin, ground
1/8 teaspoon red pepper, ground
1 garlic clove, minced
3 2/3 cups vegetable stock, divided
2 cups (1-inch) butternut squash, peeled, cubed
1 cup (1/2-inch) slices carrot
3/4 cup (1-inch) Yukon gold potato, peeled, cubed
1 tablespoon harissa
1 1/2 teaspoons tomato paste
3/4 teaspoon salt
1 lb. (450 g) turnips, peeled and each cut into 8 wedges
1 (15 1/2-ounce) can chickpeas, drained
1/4 cup fresh flat-leaf parsley, chopped
1 1/2 teaspoons honey
1 1/3 cups uncooked couscous
8 lemon wedges

7. **Directions:**

1. Add the olive oil to a large pot and set over medium-high heat.
2. Add the leek and onion and cook for 5 minutes. Add the caraway seeds, coriander, cumin, red pepper and garlic and stir-fry for a minute.

3. Add the butternut squash, carrots, potato, tomato paste, harissa, turnips and salt, pour in 3 cups of vegetable stock and bring the mixture to a boil.
4. Slow down the heat and let simmer, covered, about 30 minutes.
5. Stir in the honey and chopped parsley.
6. Take 2/3 cup hot cooking liquid from the butternut squash mixture and transfer to a medium bowl. Pour in the remaining 2/3 cup stock, as well.
7. Add the couscous, give a stir and let stand for 5 minutes, covered. Fluff the couscous with a fork.
8. Serve the stew over the cooked couscous, sprinkled with fresh cilantro leaves.
9. Serve with lemon wedges.

Moroccan Red Gazpacho

So many culinary wonders and all in your hands. Sure, you don't want to miss out this hot and spicy treat.

Prep time; 2 Hours,5 Minutes
Cook time: 5 minutes
Serves 8
8. Ingredients
1 (6 1/2-inch) pita, torn into pieces
1/2 cup boiling water
4 tablespoons extra-virgin olive oil, divided
2 tablespoons sherry vinegar

4 large ripe plum tomatoes, coarsely chopped (about 1 pound)
1 large red bell pepper, seeded and coarsely chopped
1 large cucumber, peeled, seeded, and coarsely chopped (about 8 ounces)
1/4 small yellow onion, chopped
2 cups no-salt-added tomato puree
1 cup cold water
2 teaspoons Ras el Hanout
3/4 teaspoon salt
1/2 teaspoon ground cumin
1/4 teaspoon ground cinnamon
2 tablespoons fresh cilantro, chopped

Directions:
1. Put the pita in a large shallow bowl; add 1/2 cup boiling water and let stand for 1-2 minutes.
2. Remove the moistened pita from the bowl and transfer to a food processor.
3. Add the tomatoes, cucumber, red bell pepper, sherry vinegar, 1 tablespoon oil and onion and process until smooth.
4. Add the tomato puree, water, Ras el Hanout, salt, cinnamon and cumin.
5. Refrigerate for 2 hours, covered
6. Pour the soup into serving bowls; drizzle each with 1 teaspoon oil, garnish with 3/4 teaspoon chopped cilantro.
7. Enjoy.

Moroccan Vegetable Soup

Including a great combination of healthy vegetables, this dish is a real arsenal of vitamins and nutrients.

Prep time: 15 minutes
Cook time: 55 minutes
Serves 5
Ingredients:
2 tablespoonsolive oil
1onion, chopped
1 cupcarrots,peeled, chopped
1 cupparsnips, peeled, chopped
1 cupcanned pumpkin puree
4 cupsvegetable stock
1 teaspoonlemon juice
Black pepper, ground (to taste)
Salt to taste
1/2 teaspoondried cilantro
2 teaspoonsolive oil (optional)
1 clovegarlic, minced(optional)
3 tablespoonschopped fresh parsley (optional)
1/8 teaspoonpaprika (optional)

9. Directions:
1. Add 2 tablespoons olive oil to a large saucepan and set over medium-high heat.
2. Add the onions and sauté, stirring frequently, until the onion is tender and translucent, about 5 minutes.
3. Add the parsnips and carrots, put the lid on and let cook until vegetables are crisp-tender, about 5 minutes.
4. Pour in the stock and pumpkin puree and bring the soup to a simmer over low heat, about 40 minutes. When the vegetables are soft, add the lemon juice and cilantro, and season the soup with salt and pepper.
5. Remove the saucepan from the heat and let cool.
6. Blend the soup in batches in a food processor until smooth. Add more stock if the soup is too thick.
7. Make the garnish. In a small frying pan, heat the olive oil over medium-low heat. Add the garlic and parsley and sauté for 1-

2 minutes. Stir in the paprika. Add about 1/2 teaspoon of the garnish into each serving of soup.

I love this soup. Great on a cold rainy day. I add cayenne pepper to bowl right before serving and it adds a nice heat

Moroccan Harira (Bean Soup)

If you are looking for soup with a real Moroccan flavor, then you must try Harira. The addition of beans, tomatoes and herbs makes it a healthy and tasty dish.

Prep time: 15 minutes
Cook time: 1 hr
Serves 10
Ingredients:
6 cups water
1 cup dry lentils
1 tablespoon olive oil, or to taste
1 onion, chopped
1 cinnamon stick
1 teaspoon minced fresh ginger root
1 teaspoon ground turmeric
1 teaspoon ground cumin
1 teaspoon ground black pepper
1 (15 ounce) can garbanzo beans, drained
1 (15 ounce) can red kidney beans, rinsed and drained

1 (14 ounce) can diced tomatoes
1 cup cooked quinoa (optional)
1 bunch flat-leaf parsley leaves and thinner stems, chopped
1 bunch cilantro leaves and thinner stems, chopped
1 lemon, or to taste, juiced

Directions:
1. Combine the water and lentils together in a large saucepan and set over medium-high heat.
2. Once it boils, slow down the heat to low, and let simmer.
3. Add the olive oil to a frying pan and set over medium heat.
4. Add the ginger, onion, cinnamon stick, cumin, black pepper and turmeric and sauté 1 until the onion is tender and translucent, about 5 minutes. Add this mixture to lentils mixture.
5. Add the tomatoes, quinoa, garbanzo beans and kidney beans, give a stir and continue cooking. When the mixture begins to boil, add the cilantro and parsley and let simmer over low heat until the lentils are soft, for about 45 minutes.
6. Ladle the soup into serving bowl, drizzle with lemon juice and serve.

Moroccan Spicy Sweet Potato, Carrot, and Red Lentil Soup

This spicy red lentil soup is delicious anytime. The addition of carrots and cilantro adds a nice color and fresh look to this soup.

Prep time 10 minutes
Cook time 35 minutes
Serves: 6-8

Ingredients:

2 tablespoons olive oil
1 large sweet yellow onion, chopped
1 large sweet potato, peeled and chunked
5 to 6 large carrots, peeled and chunked (about 4 cups)
1 cup red lentils
8 cups vegetable stock
1 tablespoon Harissa paste
2 teaspoons Ras el Hanout
1 teaspoon salt
1/2 teaspoon pepper
Nigella seeds (or black caraway) for garnish
Cilantro, chopped, for garnish

Directions:

1. Heat the olive oil in large griddle over moderate heat. Add the onions and sauté minutes until tender and translucent, about 7 minutes.
2. Add the carrots, potatoes, lentils, harissa paste, ras el hanout, salt and pepper, pour in the vegetable stock and bring to a boil.
3. Slow down the heat and let simmer, covered, until the lentils, potatoes and carrots are tender, 20-25 minutes. Remove from the heat and let cool.
4. Blend the soup in batches until creamy and smooth. Adjust seasonings to taste.
5. Pour the soup into serving bowls, sprinkle with chopped cilantro and Nigella seeds.
6. Enjoy.

Main Dishes

Sweet and Nutty Moroccan Couscous

Couscous is a traditional Moroccandish that has various ways of preparing it. Sure, you will enjoy this healthy version of preparation with dried apricots, dates and almonds.

Prep time: 15 minutes
Cook time: 5 minutes
Serves 6

Ingredients:
2 cups vegetable broth
5 tablespoons olive oil
1/3 cup chopped dates
1/3 cup chopped dried apricots
1/3 cup golden raisins
2 cups dry couscous
3 teaspoons ground cinnamon

1/2 cup slivered almonds, toasted

Directions:
1. Add the vegetable broth into a large pot and bring to a boil over medium-high heat.
2. Add the olive oil, dates, apricots and raisins and cook for 2-3 minutes.
3. Remove the pot from the heat, and add the couscous.
4. Put the lid on and let sit for 5 minutes.
5. Add the toasted almonds and cinnamon, stir to combine and serve.

Quinoa stuffed baby eggplants

My family adores this dish. Prepared with eggplants, quinoa and tomatoes and flavored with tons of spices, this dish cannot leave anyone indifferent. It is always a hit at the family gatherings.

Prep time: 20 minutes
Cook time: 45 minutes
Serves: 6

Ingredients:
Olive oil
1/2 tsp cloves (whole)
2-3 bay leaves
1 medium onion, chopped
1 tsp cumin seeds
1 tsp coriander powder
1/4 tsp cloves, ground
1/2 tsp cinnamon, ground
2-3 garlic cloves, minced
8-9 baby eggplants
1 cup quinoa, uncooked
1 tsp paprika
1 can of tomatoes
½ cup water
2 tablespoons sunflower seeds (or pine nuts)
1/2 cup raisins
1 cup tomato juice
1 cup water
Sea salt, to taste
Freshly ground pepper, to taste
Chili flakes

Directions:
1. Heat the olive oil in a large skillet and place over low heat. Add the cloves and bay leaves and stir-fry for 1-2 minutes, until lightly brown.
2. Remove the spices from the skillet. Add the onion, cook for about 2 minutes.
3. Then add the coriander powder, cumin seeds and cinnamon and cook over medium heat until the onion has softened.
4. Meanwhile scoop out the baby eggplant flesh and cut into small cubes.
5. Add the cubed eggplant and garlic to the skillet and sauté, stirring frequently, about 10 minutes. Add more oil, if necessary.
6. Place the tomatoes, uncooked quinoa, paprika and ½ cup water in a medium bowl and mix to combine.
7. When the eggplant is al dente, add the quinoa mix to the skillet and cook over medium heat, covered, for 5 minutes.
8. Remove the cover and let the mixture cook until the liquid is evaporated and the quinoa is crisp-tender.
9. Remove the skillet from the heat, and add the raisins and sunflower seeds sprinkle the stuffing with chili flakes and salt and pepper.
10. Fill the eggplants with the stuffing and cover with their own stems.
11. Gently place them in a Dutch oven, tightly close to each other, so they stay upright. Add 1 cup tomato juice, 1 cup water, sprinkle some olive oil over the eggplants and cook over medium heat, about 20 minutes, until the quinoa is tender.

Sweet Potato, Chickpea and Zucchini Tagine

This is an authentic dish that tastes like it came straight from a five star Moroccan restaurant! Serve it hot over couscous and enjoy.

Prep time: 10 minutes
Cook time: 35 minutes
Serves: 4

Ingredients:
2 sweet potatoes, peeled and cubed
1 zucchini, chopped
14 oz. (400g) tin of chickpeas, drained and rinsed
2 green bell peppers
1 large onion, chopped
4 cloves of garlic, finely chopped
1 tablespoon of ginger, peeled and grated
2 teaspoons sweet paprika
2 teaspoons of smoked paprika
2 teaspoons ground coriander
2 teaspoons ground cumin
1 teaspoon chili powder
1 teaspoon cinnamon
½ teaspoon ground cardamom
½ teaspoon allspice
3 tablespoons of olive oil
1 cup of vegetable stock
¼ cup of apricots, chopped
¼ cup of fresh coriander, chopped
Flaked or slivered almonds to serve

Directions:
1. Preheat the oven to 450 °F (230 °C)
2. Place the sweet potato and 1 tablespoon of olive oil in a bowl and toss to coat.
3. Transfer to a rimmed baking pan.
4. Place the bell peppers in a roasting pan. Place both pans in the oven and bake for 25- 30 minutes, until the sweet potato is soft when pierced with a fork and the bell peppers become light brown.
5. Let cool. Remove the skin of bell peppers and chop peppers into thin strips.
6. Place a large casserole dish over medium-high heat. Add the olive oil, garlic, onion, ginger, and spices. Sauté until the onions are tender and golden-brown and the spices are fragrant.
7. Stir in the zucchini and cook until just-tender.
8. Stir in the sweet potato, apricots, the vegetable stock, chickpeas, and green peppers and bring the mixture to a boil.
9. Slow down the heat and let simmer for 8-10 minutes.
10. Pour the tagine into serving bowls, sprinkle with chopped coriander and almonds.
11. Enjoy

Vegan Moroccan Stuffed Squash

This recipe makes an authentic Moroccan dish, perfect for lunch and dinner. Carrots, chickpeas, squash and onion, as well as fresh dries apricots and nuts make this dish healthy and full of flavor.

Prep time: 15 minutes
Cook time: 70 minutes
Serves 4-6
Ingredients;
2 large squash (butternut, small pumpkin)
2 medium (150 g) tomatoes diced
1 medium carrot peeled, thinly chopped
1 cup (150 g)chickpeas, cooked/canned, drained
1/2 cup hazelnuts or walnuts, chopped
1/4 cup dried apricots, chopped
3 tablespoons olive oil
1 medium onion, chopped
2 cloves garlic finely chopped

1/2 teaspoon fresh ginger finely, chopped
1/2 teaspoon black pepper
1/2 teaspoon paprika
1/2 teaspoon ground cinnamon or 1-2 small sticks cinnamon bark
1 teaspoon turmeric
3/4 teaspoon salt
2 1/2 cups vegetable stock or water + 2 tablespoons vegetable broth powder
1 cup couscous (uncooked)

Directions:
1. Preheat oven to 400°F (200°C). Lightly coat a baking sheet with oil.
2. Halve the squash in lengthwise. Using a spoon, remove soft insides and arrange on the baking sheet, hollowed side up.
3. Roast in the oven for 20 minutes.
4. Sauté the garlic, onion, ginger, nuts, paprika and pepper in the heated oil over moderate heat about 3 minutes.
5. Stir in the tomatoes, chickpeas, carrots, apricots / raisins, turmeric and cinnamon and cook for another 3 minutes.
6. Add the vegetable broth powder, salt, vegetable stock or water and bring the mixture to a boil. Let cook for 5 minutes stirring constantly.
7. Add the couscous and bring to a simmer over low heat, stirring frequently, until the couscous is tender, 6-7 minutes.
8. Once the squash halves are done, remove from the oven and fill with vegetable couscous stuffing.
9. Bake the stuffed squash in the oven until squash is done, about 30-35 minutes.
10. Garnish the dish with chopped fresh parsley and chopped nuts, season with ground paprika and serve.

Vegan Moroccan Tagine

This dish is a vegan version of tagine, full of healthy vegetables and flavors that work together well and create a tasty and hearty meal. Serve it with bread or couscous and enjoy.

Prep time: 20 minutes
Cooking time: 30 minutes
Serves 4

Ingredients:
1 cup garbanzo beans, cooked
1 small eggplant, diced
1 red bell pepper, diced
1 medium zucchini, sliced
1 large potato, peeled and diced
1 large onion, sliced
1 cup sliced mushrooms
1 carrot, peeled and diced
3 medium tomatoes, pureed
4 cloves garlic, minced

¼ cup fresh parsley, roughly chopped
¼ cup golden raisins or sultanas
2 tablespoons olive oil
1 tablespoon ground cumin,
½ tbsp coriander, ground
3 tsp sugar
Cinnamon stick
Sea salt
Dried red chili flakes (optional)

Directions:
1. Heat the olive oil in a large saucepan over medium-high heat.
2. Add onion and garlic and sauté for 1-2 minutes. Add the cinnamon stick and sauté until fragrant.
3. Add the carrot, potato, red pepper, raisins, eggplant, and zucchini. Season with salt and cook for 3 to 4 minutes, stirring frequently.
4. Heat some olive oil in another pan and sauté mushrooms for a couple of minutes. Add to the vegetables.
5. Add the cumin and coriander and stir well.
6. Stir in the garbanzo beans, tomato puree and sugar, put the lid on and cook for 5 minutes over low heat. Once the vegetables are crisp-tender, add the chopped parsley and let cook for another 3-4 minutes, covered.
7. Remove from the heat and let stand 15 minutes before serving.

Couscous Shepherd's Pie

This dish is perfect for any gathering. The combination of couscous, carrots and Ras el hanout promise an interesting experience.

Prep time: 10 minutes
Cook time: 1hr 25 minutes
Serves 8

Ingredients:
4 tablespoons olive oil, divided
1 small onion, thinly sliced (1 cup)
3–4 tablespoons ras el hanout
2 15-oz. cans crushed tomatoes
4 carrots, cut (1 cup)
1 turnip, cut (1 cup)
2 zucchini, cut (1 cup)
1 ½ cups cooked chickpeas, or 1 15-oz. can chickpeas, rinsed and drained, divided
1 ½ cups couscous
1 tsp. salt

Directions:
1. Add 2 tablespoons of oil to a saucepan and set over medium heat. Add the onion, and cook 5 minutes, until tender.
2. Add Ras el Hanout, and cook1 minute, or until it becomes brown.
3. Add 3 cups water and tomatoes, season with salt and pepper and bring to a simmer over medium-low heat, 18-20 minutes.
4. Stir in the turnip and carrots, put the lid on and cook about 10 minutes.
5. Add 3/4 cup chickpeas and zucchini and cook for another 5 minutes.
6. Place the remaining 3/4 cup chickpeas in a blender and pulse until puree. Combine with the vegetable mixture, season with salt and pepper.
7. Transfer the vegetable mixture to a 13 x 9-inch baking dish.

8. Preheat oven to 350°F (175 °C). Place the couscous and salt in large heat-proof bowl, pour in 3 cups of boiling water, and let stand 5-10 minutes, until all water is absorbed.
9. Fluff the couscous with fork, and add the remaining 2 tablespoons oil.
10. Spoon the couscous over vegetable mixture and spread evenly.
11. Bake in the oven, until golden on top, about 25- 30 minutes.

Sweet Moroccan Glazed Tofu

This is an absolutely delicious dish and is perfect for any time of the day! Sure, it will make you a tofu lover once you try it.

Prep time: 7 minutes
Cook time: 7 minutes
Serves 4

Ingredients:

12 oz (330 g). Extra-firmtofu drained and pressed
1 teaspoon black pepper
1 teaspoon paprika
1 teaspoon salt
1/2 teaspoon cumin
1/4 teaspoon allspice
1 cup vegetable broth
1 medium carrot, chopped
1/2 cup frozen peas
1 tsp. olive oil
3/4 cup couscous
2 tbsp. canola oil
1/4 cup agave syrup

Directions:
1. Thinly slice the tofu and put them onto a large plate.
2. Combine the allspice, paprika, cumin, salt and pepper in a small bowl and sprinkle over the tofu, so it is evenly coated.
3. Add the peas, carrots, olive oil and vegetable broth to a large pot and bring to a boil. Stir in the couscous, season with 1/2 tsp salt and remove the pot from the heat.
4. Let stand for about 5 minutes, until all liquid is absorbed.
5. Add the agave and canola oil to a skillet and set over medium-high heat. Once it bubbles, add the sliced tofu, spiced side down and cook for 3-4 minutes.
6. Gently turn over to cook the other side, too, 3 minutes more.
7. Fluff the couscous with a fork. Transfer it to a serving bowl and top with the done tofu.
8. Enjoy.

Vegan Berber Pizza

This is a vegan version for Medfouna. It is a Berber flatbread, stuffed with olives, herbs, onions and lots of spices

Prep Time: 30 minutes
Cook Time: 25 minutes
Serves 4-6

Ingredients
4 cups flour (some wheat, if desired)
2 teaspoons salt
2 teaspoons sugar
2 tablespoons olive oil
1 tablespoon yeast
1 1/4 cups warm water
For the Filling
2 lbs. (about 900 g) onions, chopped
1 bell pepper (any color), chopped
2 tablespoons olive oil
1 to 1 1/2 cups pitted green olives, sliced
2 handfuls of fresh parsley, chopped
2 tablespoons fresh thyme
1 teaspoon paprika
1 teaspoon cumin
1 teaspoon ground coriander
1/2 teaspoon ground red pepper (or to taste)
Salt and pepper (to taste)
1/2 teaspoon sugar (optional)
Olive oil,
Salt
Herbs for garnish (optional)

Directions:
1. In a large bowl, combine the flour, salt and sugar. In the center of the flour mixture, make a large hole and add the yeast.
2. Pour also the water and olive oil into the hole, and mix with a whisk, until the yeast is dissolved.
3. Then the dough is formed, transfer it to working surface, dusted with flour and knead with hands to make smooth and elastic dough.
4. Shape 2 balls, coat their surface with olive oil and let rise for about 40-45 minutes, covered with kitchen towel.
5. Start making the filling. Add the olive to a large frying pan and heat over medium heat.
6. Add the bell pepper and onions and cook until the onions have just softened, about 7 minutes. Remove the pan onions from the heat. Add the olives, herbs and spices, mix well and set aside.
7. Preheat an oven to 435°F (225°C).
8. Using a rolling pin, roll out one ball of the risen dough into a large round. Coat a baking sheet with oil and place the dough onto it.
9. Spoon the onion filling in the center, and spread evenly leaving at least 1/2" of dough exposed all around. Brush the exposed edge of dough with a little water.
10. Roll out the second ball of dough into round and put over the filling.
11. Lightly press the edges of the dough until sealed. Coat the dough with olive oil, season with salt and herbs.
12. Bake in the oven until golden brown, about 20 minutes. Transfer to a rack and let cool slightly. Serve warm.

Desserts

Oranges with Caramel and Cardamom Syrup

Cardamom pods and orange-flower water make this dessert so flavorful, moist and light that one can hardly stand the wish of taking the second portion.

Prep time: 35 minutes
Cook time: 12 minutes
6 servings

Ingredients:
1/2 cup water
2 cardamom pods, crushed
6 tablespoons sugar
5 medium navel oranges
2 tablespoons honey
1/8 teaspoon orange-flower water
Mint sprigs (optional)

Directions:
1. Add the cardamom and 1/2 cup water to a small heavy pot and set over medium-high heat.
2. Once the mixture boils, remove the pot from the heat and let stand, covered, for about 25 minutes.
3. Strain the mixture through a fine sieve and discard solids.
4. Add 1 tablespoon cardamom water and sugar to a skillet and place over medium heat. Cook for 7-8 minutes until sugar is melted and golden, without stirring.
5. Increase the heat to medium-high, and cook for another minute until the mixture becomes dark.
6. Remove from heat; gently pour the remaining cardamom water into the skillet and set back over medium-high heat, stirring constantly.
7. Using a paring knife, peel the oranges and cut crosswise into 6 slices each.
8. Place the slices on a rimmed dish and spoon hot syrup over oranges.
9. Refrigerate overnight, covered.
10. In a small bowl combine the honey and orange-flower water.
11. Garnish the oranges with mint sprigs and serve with honey mixture.

Moroccan Peaches

This is really a very amazing delicacy, which might become one of your favorites for treating your Moroccan guests.

Prep Time: 10 minutes
Cook Time: 2 hrs
Servings: 8

Ingredients:
8 largepeaches, ripe
3 tablespoonssuperfine sugar
8 teaspoonsrose water
Fresh mint leaves, to decorate

Directions:
1. Using a paring knife, peel the peaches and remove the pit. Cut each peach into 4-6 wedges and transfer to a serving bowl.
2. Spoon the rosewater over the peaches, sprinkle with sugar and place the bowl into the refrigerator for 2 hours, covered.
3. Garnish the peaches with mint leaves and enjoy.

Moroccan Apple Dessert

Only the taste of these apples, flavored with cinnamon, lemons and orange blossom water worth the time spent in the kitchen.

Prep Time: 20 minutes
Cook Time: 15 minutes
Servings: 6-8

Ingredients:

8 tart apples, peeled cored and sliced in 8-10 wedges
3 lemons
2 cups sugar
2 cups water
2 tablespoons cinnamon
2 -4 tablespoons orange blossom water

Directions:

1. Peel the lemon and slice the rind into thin strips.
2. Juice the peeled lemons and reserve 1/2 cup of juice for later use.
3. Remove the peel and core from the apples and cut each into 8 to10 wedges.
4. Add the water, sugar, and cinnamon to a large pot and set over moderate heat.
5. Once it boils, stir in the lemon rind, apples, orange blossom water and lemon juice.
6. Let the mixture cook until the lemon rind and apples are soft and all liquid has evaporated.
7. Remove the pot from heat and let stand for 30 minutes before serving.

Moroccan Charoset Balls

Making these charosetballsis a real party for whole family. Make sure the kids are not around, as they will eat out all the balls before your guests arrive. Chill them for a while and enjoy.

Prep Time: 1 hr 15 minutes
Cook Time: 0 minutes
Serves 3-4
Ingredients:
2 cupspitted dates
1/2cupgolden raisin
1/2cupdark raisin
1/2cupwalnuts
1 -2 tablespoonsweet red wine

Directions:
1. Place the raisins, dates, walnuts in a food processor and pulse until finely chopped.
2. Add the wine and blend to get a sticky paste.
3. Place rounded teaspoonfuls of paste onto a baking sheet lined with wax paper.
4. Moisten your hands and roll each portion into a 1-inch ball.
5. Chill for 1-2 hours before serving.

Moroccan Cinnamon Cookies – Montecaos

Enjoy these extremely delicious and gorgeous looking cinnamon cookies with a cup of Moroccan mint tea.

Prep time: 10 minutes
Cook time: 20 minutes
Serves: 60

Ingredients:

1 cup vegetable oil
1⅓ cup confectioner's sugar
2 cups almond flour
2 cups whole wheat pastry flour
¼ tsp. salt
½ tsp. baking powder
1 tbsp. cinnamon

Directions:
1. Preheat oven at 325 °F (160 °C).
2. Place the sugar and oil in a large bowl and whisk well until the sugar is dissolved. Whisk in the almond flour.
3. In another bowl, place together the flour, baking powder, cinnamon and salt, slightly mix and add to the sugar mixture. Using a wooden spoon, mix well. Then knead the mixture with hands to form elastic dough.
4. Shape 60 small balls and arrange on the baking sheet, lined with parchment.
5. Bake in the preheated oven for 20 minutes until golden. Remove from the oven and let cool. Sprinkle the cookies with cinnamon and serve.

Sfenj-Moroccan Doughnuts

These simple doughnuts are a favorite treat in Morocco. I usually divide the dough, fry half of the doughnuts, and refrigerate the rest always to make a fresh treat. Coated with granulated sugar they make a great weekend breakfast.

Prep time: 1 hr 15 minutes
Cook time: 20 minutes
Makes 40 small doughnuts

Ingredients:
2.2lbs (I kg) all purpose flour
1 oz. (25 g) active dry yeast
3 1/3 cups lukewarm water
2/3 cup sugar
1 teaspoon salt
Canola oil for deep frying
Bit of canola oil for forming the dough
Sugar for coating

Directions:
1. Combine the yeast, sugar and water in small bowl and mix well.
2. In a large bowl, mix together the flour and salt.
3. Pour in the yeast mixture and knead well with your hands to get sticky dough. Cover the bowl with plastic wrap and place in a warm corner to rise for 1-2 hours until the dough doubles or triples its volume.
4. Add the canola oil to a large griddle and set over moderate heat. Once sizzling. Coat your hands with oil and take plum size dough .Using your index finger make a hole in the ball of dough and stretch the hole wide to make a ring.
5. Transfer the dough to the hot griddle and fry for about 2-3 minutes per side until golden. Transfer to paper towels to drain.
6. Repeat the process with the remaining dough.
7. Coat the doughnuts with granulated sugar and serve immediately.

Moroccan Sesame Seed cookies

These sesame seed cookies are easy to make and taste delicious. Serve them with fresh made fruit salad and satisfy your sweet tooth in the healthiest way.

Prep time: 30 minutes
Cook time: 25 minutes
Makes 36 cookies

Ingredients:
3 cups sesame seeds
2 ½ cups flour
1 cup vegetable oil
1 cup water
1 cup granulated sugar
1 teaspoon vanilla
1 ½ teaspoons baking powder

Directions:

1. Combine the flour, sugar, sesame seeds and vanilla in a large bowl.
2. Add the oil and mix well. Then gradually add the water and continue mixing until smooth and a bit sticky.
3. Preheat the oven to 325 °F (165 °C). Line a baking sheet with parchment.
4. Split the dough into 3 balls and chill for 25 minutes.
5. Roll out the dough into a thin rectangle on a piece of parchment paper. Cut the dough into cookie shapes with a cookie cutter. Repeat this with the remaining balls.
6. Arrange the cookies on the baking sheet and bake in the oven for 22-25 minutes until lightly golden.

Moroccan Date Bonbons

These amazing bonbons are flavored with tons of spices and healthy nuts. Coat them with pistachio powder to make the chef-d'oeuvre complete.

Prep time: 25 minutes
Cook time: 4 minutes
Makes 30 bonbons

Ingredients:
- 1/2 cup plus 2 tablespoons sliced almonds
- 1/2 cup shelled pistachios
- 3/4 cup chopped walnuts
- 1 pound moist pitted dates, chopped
- 4 pitted kalamata or dry-cured Moroccan olives, chopped
- 1/2 tablespoon finely grated fresh ginger
- 1/2 tablespoon honey
- 1/2 teaspoon orange zest, finely grated
- 1/4 teaspoon cinnamon
- 1/8 teaspoon ground cardamom
- 1/8 teaspoon orange flower water
- 1/8 teaspoon salt

Directions:
1. Preheat the oven to 350°F (170 °C). Place the sliced almonds on a baking tray and toast for about 3-4 minutes, until fragrant and golden. Let cool completely.
2. Place the pistachios in a food processor and pulse until coarsely ground.
3. Remove the ground pistachio from the food processor and grind the toasted almonds in the processor.
4. Add the dates, walnuts, olives, ginger, orange zest, honey, cardamom, cinnamon, orange flower water and salt and pulse until paste.
5. Moisten your hands and shape about 30 balls. Gently roll the bonbons in the pistachio powder until evenly coated.
6. Enjoy.

Honey Almond Stuffed Dates

One-two steps and these wonderful honey almond dates are ready to be served. They will create a pleasant atmosphere along with a cup of tea or coffee.

Prep time: 5 minutes
Cook time: 10 minutes
Makes 20 filled dates

Ingredients:

20 dates
20 almonds
2 tsp honey

Directions:
1. Place the almonds in a small skillet and toast over medium-low heat until fragrant and light golden, 3-4 minutes.
2. Remove from the heat and stir in the honey. Return the skillet back to the heat and let cook until almonds are caramelized, 5 minutes.
3. Place still hot almonds onto a piece of baking parchment and gently with a fork. Let cool.
4. Halve the dates in lengthways and remove the pit. Place a sticky almond in the hole of each date and gently press the date on both sides with fingers.

Conclusion

I believe that with this cookbook we could transfer you the real spirit of Moroccan cuisine, to feel the real color and flavor of Morocco. With a basic knowledge of cooking tweaks and techniques, you can prepare healthy vegan soups, salads, stews or desserts and enjoy at the table with your family.

If you went through the recipes and had a chance to taste them you have noticed that Moroccan cuisine is rich in fresh vegetables, fruits, grains, olive oil, beans, herbs and spices and it offers wide variety of options for vegan people, or for those who intend to increase vegetables in their diet.

Thank you once again for choosing this cookbook and good luck.

HEALTHY VEGAN GREEK RECIPES

BY <u>BRYAN RYLEE</u>

DISCLAIMER:
THE INFORMATION PRESENTED IN THIS BOOK REPRESENTS THE VIEWS OF THE PUBLISHER AS OF THE DATE OF PUBLICATION. THE PUBLISHER RESERVES THE RIGHTS TO ALTER UPDATE THEIR OPINIONS BASED ON NEW CONDITIONS. THIS REPORT IS FOR INFORMATIONAL PURPOSES ONLY. THE AUTHOR AND THE PUBLISHER DO NOT ACCEPT ANY RESPONSIBILITIES FOR ANY LIABILITIES RESULTING FROM THE USE OF THIS INFORMATION. WHILE EVERY ATTEMPT HAS BEEN MADE TO VERIFY THE INFORMATION PROVIDED HERE, THE AUTHOR AND THE PUBLISHER CANNOT ASSUME ANY RESPONSIBILITY FOR ERRORS, INACCURACIES OR OMISSIONS. ANY SIMILARITIES WITH PEOPLE OR FACTS ARE UNINTENTIONAL.

TABLE OF CONTENTS

Introduction 5

The Greek Vegan Cuisine – Most Common Ingredients 9
Appetizers 12
Corn and Garbanzo Bean Patties 12
(Vegan) 12
Greek Style Hummus 18
Eggplant Purée with Walnuts..............................20
Briam (Greek potato and zucchini bake)..............24
Rice-Stuffed Tomatoes..26
Salads 29
Greek Bulgur Salad 29
Traditional Greek Potato Salad (Patatosalata) 33
Cabbage Salad (Lahanosalata) 36
Greek Couscous Salad with Avocado................40
Greek Vegan Salad..42
Soups and stews 44
Greek Potato Stew..44
Fasolada..46
Cabbage Soup...48
Manestra (Orzo Soup)..50
Spicy Greek Pumpkin Soup 50
Greek Stew with Green Beans and Potato..........52
Fasolakia (Green Bean Stew)..............................54
Greek Chickpeas with Spinach 56
The combination of spinach and lemon juice is fantastic. Give a try and this stew will become your favorite................56
Pureed Split Pea Soup 58
Greek Mains...60
Orzo with Zucchini 60
Greek Vegetables 64
Dolmades (Stuffed Grape Leaves) 65

Greek Vegan pasta 68
Braised Eggplant with Potatoes 70
Quinoa Mushroom Pilaf 72
Desserts 73
Fluffy Blueberry Waffles 73
Peach Barley 83
Greek Lenten Cake 85

Introduction

I WANT TO THANK YOU AND CONGRATULATE YOU ON CHOOSING THE BOOK, "HEALTHY VEGAN GREEK RECIPES".
THE MERE FACT THAT YOU ARE READING THIS BOOK MEANS YOU HAVE MADE A DECISION THAT WILL CHANGE YOUR LIFESTYLE – A CHANGE THAT WILL MAKE YOU HEALTHIER AND HAPPIER. YOU MUST HAVE READ A HUNDRED TIMES THAT HEALTHY EATING HABITS HAVE A POSITIVE EFFECT, NOT ONLY ON YOUR WEIGHT AND HEALTH, BUT ALSO YOUR OPTIMISTIC ATTITUDE TO WHATEVER IS HAPPENING AROUND. AND THIS BOOK IS NOT AN EXCEPTION. IT WILL GUIDE YOU THROUGH THE PROCESS OF PREPARING HEALTHY AND TASTY GREEK VEGAN DISHES WITH INGREDIENTS THAT ARE EASY TO FIND AND COOK. YOU WILL FIND A WIDE RANGE OF RECIPES, WHICH CAN BE ADAPTED FOR A HEALTHY BREAKFAST AND A HEARTY LUNCH, AND SOME THAT WILL GO WELL AS A DINNER OR A LIGHT SUPPER. WE HAVE INCLUDED A LARGE ASSORTMENT OF DELICIOUS DESSERTS AND SNACKS. THE RECIPES PROVIDE A STEP-BY-STEP DESCRIPTION OF HOW TO COOK HEALTHY AND, AT THE SAME TIME, TASTY FOOD, INCLUDING SOUPS AND STEWS MADE OF LEGUMES, VEGETABLES AND GREENS.

THE SELECTION OF GREEK VEGAN CUISINE RECIPES IS INITIALLY CONDITIONED WITH A LARGE VARIETY OF VEGETABLES AND HERBS, GRAINS, WINE, FISH AND OTHER INGREDIENTS. AS IN EVERY SIMILAR CUISINE, OLIVE OIL IS ONE OF THE KEY ELEMENTS OF GREEK FOODS. IT IS SIMPLY AN OUTSTANDING REFLECTION OF TRADITIONAL MEDITERRANEAN CUISINE CONTAINING A HIGH LEVEL OF NUTRIENTS AND A LOW AMOUNT OF ANIMAL FATS. THE POPULARITY OF GREEK CUISINE,

PARTICULARLY VEGAN CUISINE, HAS TO DO WITH ITS HISTORY, GEOGRAPHY AND CLIMATE ALLOWING THE ABILITY TO CULTIVATE DIFFERENT TYPES OF FRUITS, VEGETABLES AND GRAINS. ALTHOUGH GREEK CUISINE HAD BEEN AFFECTED BY ROMAN, BYZANTIUM, TURKISH AND OTHER CULTURES, IT HAS STILL PRESERVED ITS UNIQUENESS.

AS MENTIONED, OLIVE OIL PLAYS A MAIN ROLE IN GREEK VEGAN CUISINE, IT IS PRESENT IN MANY DISHES. VEGETABLES ALSO PLAY AN IMPORTANT ROLE IN THE CUISINE, THE MAIN VEGETABLES INCLUDE TOMATOES, EGGPLANT, GREEN BEANS, GREEN PEPPER, ONIONS AND OKRA. GREEK COOKING OFTEN CALLS FOR STUFFING VEGETABLES. THE MOST FAMOUS DISH IS *TOMATES GEMISTA*, STUFFED TOMATOES WITH RICE, ONIONS, HERBS AND MEAT. GREECE HAS A HUGE VARIETY OF APPETIZERS AND SALADS MADE FROM FRESH VEGETABLES AND FRUIT. ANYONE WHO HAS VISITED GREECE AT LEAST ONCE MUST HAVE TRIED THE FAMOUS GREEK SALAD WHICH IS MADE FROM FRESH RIPE RED TOMATOES, ONIONS, CUCUMBERS, GREEN PEPPERS, OLIVES, OLIVE OIL, FETA CHEESE (IF NOT VEGAN) AND OREGANO. WITH SO MANY KINDS OF VEGETABLES GREECE IS A REAL PARADISE FOR PEOPLE FOLLOWING THE VEGAN DIET.

GREECE IS ALSO WELL KNOWN FOR ITS VARIOUS HERBS AND SPICES, SO IT IS NOT SURPRISING THAT GREEK MEALS ARE SO TASTY AND FLAVORFUL. HERBS AND SPICES CAN BE USED FLAKED OR WHOLE, FRESH OR DRIED, AS LEAVES OR STEMS, AS SEEDS, AND IN OTHER VARIATIONS. THE MOST POPULAR AMONG THESE ARE OREGANO, MINT, GARLIC, ONION, DILL AND BAY LAUREL LEAVES.

FRUITS ARE ALSO AN IMPORTANT STAPLE IN THE GREEK DIET. TYPICALLY, A BOWL OF FRESH FRUIT IS

SERVED WITH ALMOST EVERY MEAL. YOU CAN EAT EITHER FRESH OR DRIED FRUITS, SUCH AS PLUMS, APRICOTS, APPLES, GRAPES, FIGS, DATES, AND CHERRIES. GREEK COOKING ALSO HAS THE TRADITION OF BAKING OR ROASTING FRUITS IN THE OVEN. IN THIS BOOK YOU CAN FIND SOME WONDERFUL RECIPES INCORPORATING BAKED FRUIT.

THE OTHER CONSISTENT INGREDIENT OF THE GREEK VEGAN CUISINE IS WHEAT. THIS IS A NATIONAL STAPLE PRODUCT, ONE THAT IS FOUND IN MANY RECIPES, AND IT HAS BEEN CULTIVATED IN GREECE FOR THOUSANDS OF YEARS. IT'S USED IN THE PREPARATION OF DIFFERENT TYPES OF FOODS, SUCH AS BREAD, NAMELY IN THE WELL KNOWN PITA BREAD. BULGUR, MADE OF CRACKED WHOLE WHEAT, CAN BE EATEN SEPARATELY OR ADDED INTO SOUPS OR SALADS.

THE FINAL TYPICAL GRAIN FOOD OF GREEK VEGAN COOKING IS RICE. THIS IS USED IN PILAFS AND BAKES, SERVED WITH STEWS, OR WRAPPED IN GRAPE LEAVES TO MAKE DOLMADES.

The Greek Vegan Cuisine – Most Common Ingredients

THE OLIVE - OLIVES ARE USED IN COOKING IN MANY COUNTRIES, BUT THE MOST POPULAR OLIVE IN THE WORLD ARE THE ALMOND SIZED BLACK OLIVES, KALAMATA, WHICH HAVE A RICH AND FRUITY TASTE. THE COLOR OF THE OLIVES DEPENDS ON THE SEASON DURING WHICH THEY WERE CROPPED. IN GREECE YOU CAN OFTEN FIND OLIVES STUFFED WITH GARLIC, WILD FENNEL, LEMON OR HOT PEPPER FLAKES. IN GREECE OLIVES ARE ALSO EATEN WHOLE. KALAMATA AND OTHER DARK OLIVES ARE STORED EITHER IN VINEGAR OR IN OLIVE OIL. OLIVES PROVIDE AN EXCELLENT AND IMPRESSIVE TANG TO MANY DISHES, FROM VEGETABLE SALADS TO MEAT SAUCES.

OLIVE OIL - ONE CANNOT IMAGINE GREEK CUISINE WITHOUT OLIVE OIL. IT IS RICH IN MINERALS AND VITAMINS. GREEK OLIVE OIL, MAINLY THE EXTRA VIRGIN OIL, IS IN GREAT DEMAND AS GREEK PEOPLE MAKE THE WORLD'S BEST OLIVE OIL. EXTRA VIRGIN OIL IS OBTAINED IN THE PROCESS OF FIRST PRESSING OF THE OLIVES; IT IS UNREFINED AND HAS A MILDER AND A MORE DELICATE TASTE. IN GREEK CUISINE OLIVE OIL IS THE MAIN COOKING FAT. IT IS USED IN COOKING OF SOUPS AND STEWS, FOR FLAVORING SALADS, AND EVEN IN BAKING.

BEANS AND LEGUMES - BEANS AND LEGUMES ARE AN IMPORTANT PART OF GREEK COOKING. BEANS ARE A GOOD SOURCE OF FIBER AND PROTEINS, AND THEY ALSO HELP TO LOWER CHOLESTEROL LEVEL IN BLOOD. BEANS ARE ALSO A PERFECT FOOD FOR PEOPLE TRYING TO LOSE WEIGHT, AS EATING SMALL PORTIONS

KEEPS YOU FULL FOR A LONG TIME. ALONG WITH OTHER LEGUMES, SUCH AS LENTILS, CHICKPEAS AND SPLIT PEAS, BEANS ARE USED IN SOUPS AND SALADS, AS WELL AS IN STEWED, ROASTED MEALS AND PATTIES.

LEMON - THIS IS WIDELY USED IN GREEK COOKING AND IS ONE OF THE DEFINING FLAVORS. GREEKS USE LEMON JUICE IN ALMOST EVERY DISH. THEY SQUEEZE FRESH LEMON OVER BEAN SALADS, GRILLED MEATS, GRILLED CHICKEN KEBABS AND GREEN SALADS. LEMON ZEST AND JUICES ARE ALSO A DELICIOUS ADDITION TO SWEETS AND DESSERTS, PROVIDING A PLEASANT SAVORY TASTE.

CINNAMON - THIS IS A VERY POPULAR SPICE IN GREECE. GREEK PEOPLE USE CINNAMON IN PREPARING CAKES, COOKIES AND CANDIES, AS WELL AS WHEN MARINATING MEAT AND FISH. THIS SPICE ADDS A UNIQUE TASTE TO ANY FOOD.
OREGANO - THIS IS THE MOST WIDELY USED HERB IN THE GREEK CUISINE. IT IS MOSTLY USED WITH MEAT, SALADS (ESPECIALLY IN THE FAMOUS GREEK SALAD), IN TOMATO SAUCES, FISH AND EGG DISHES, AND WITH CHEESE, AS WELL AS WITH VARIOUS VEGETABLES AND LEGUMES. IN GREECE YOU MAY COME ACROSS OREGANO ON THE TABLE TOGETHER WITH SALT AND PEPPER. DRINKING OREGANO TEA IS RECOMMENDED AGAINST COUGHS AND INDIGESTION.

WILD GREENS - WILD GREENS ARE VERY POPULAR IN THE GREEK CUISINE. THEY ARE USED RAW, BOILED AND BAKED IN CASSEROLES. THEY ARE USUALLY SERVED SPRINKLED WITH LEMON JUICE AND OLIVE OIL. WILD GREENS ARE RICH IN VITAMINS AND MINERALS, AS WELL AS ALSO BEING HIGH IN ANTI-OXIDANTS. ONE OF THE MOST COMMON GREENS IN GREEK COOKING IS SPINACH, THIS IS USED BOTH FRESH AND FROZEN. WHEN RAW, SPINACH HAS A MUCH MILDER TASTE THAN AFTER IT HAD BEEN COOKED.
GREEN HERBS - HERBS ARE A KEY INGREDIENT IN THE GREEK CUISINE, AND HAVE BEEN USED IN GREECE FROM ANCIENT TIMES. CILANTRO, PARSLEY, MINT, AND GREEN DILL ARE THE MAIN GREEN HERBS USED IN COOKING. THEY PROVIDE A FRESH AND UNIQUE FLAVOR TO ANY DISH. THEY ARE ALSO GREAT SOURCES OF VITAMINS AND ANTIOXIDANTS.

Appetizers
Corn and Garbanzo Bean Patties
(Vegan)

THESE FANTASTIC PATTIES CAN BE SERVED WITH ANY MAIN COURSE. THEY ARE VERY TASTY AND AROMATIC. THE BEANS PROVIDE A HIGH PROTEIN CONTENT, SO THIS DISH CAN BE EASILY INTEGRATED INTO YOUR HEALTHY DIET.
PREPARATION TIME 2 MINUTES
COOKING TIME 8 MINUTES
SERVES: 6

INGREDIENTS:
1 TSP CANOLA OIL
1 TBSP CANOLA OIL
1½ CUPS FRESH OR FROZEN CORN KERNELS (THAWED)
2 TBSP SHALLOTS, CHOPPED
½ TSP GREEK OREGANO

2 TSP FRESH ITALIAN PARSLEY, MINCED
1 19OZ (230G) CAN GARBANZO BEANS, DRAINED
1 CUP FRESH BREADCRUMBS
2 TBSP FINE GRAIN CORNMEAL, OR 2 TABLESPOONS MASA HARINA
½ TSP SALT
2 TBSP RED BELL PEPPERS, MINCED
1 TBSP POLENTA (COARSE CORNMEAL)

DRESSING
¼ CUP FRESH LEMON JUICE
⅓ CUP EXTRA VIRGIN OLIVE OIL
SALT, TO TASTE
FRESH GROUND BLACK PEPPER, TO TASTE

GARNISH
5OZ (150G) ARUGULA LEAVES OR MIXED GREENS (RINSED, DRAINED)
FRESH GARLIC CHIVES, MINCED

DIRECTIONS:
1. ADD 1 TEASPOON OF OLIVE OIL TO A LARGE SKILLET AND SET OVER A MEDIUM-HIGH HEAT. STIR IN THE SHALLOTS, CORN AND OREGANO, AND COOK FOR A COUPLE OF MINUTES. REMOVE FROM THE HEAT AND LET IT COOL. ADD THE FRESH PARSLEY AND STIR TO COMBINE.
2. PLACE THE CORNMEAL, GARBANZO BEANS, 2 TABLESPOONS OF THE RESERVED GARBANZO BEAN LIQUID, BREAD CRUMBS, MINCED RED BELL PEPPER AND SALT INTO A BLENDER. PROCESS UNTIL COARSELY GROUND.
3. ADD THE FRIED CORN AND SHALLOT MIXTURE TO THE BLENDED MIXTURE, AND ADD ANOTHER TABLESPOON OF THE BEAN LIQUID AND BLEND (8-10 TIMES) UNTIL FINELY GROUND.
4. MOISTEN YOUR HANDS AND SHAPE THE MIXTURE INTO 6 PATTIES. GENTLY COAT THE PATTIES WITH POLENTA AND FRY IN THE REMAINING TABLESPOON OF OLIVE OIL OVER A MEDIUM TO HIGH HEAT. COOK THE PATTIES IN BATCHES, 3 AT A TIME. LET THEM COOK FOR 3-4 MINUTES PER SIDE, THEN TURN TO BROWN ON THE OTHER SIDE.
5. PLACE THE DONE PATTIES IN THE OVEN AT

200°F (100°C) TO KEEP WARM. MAKE THE DRESSING BY COMBINING THE FRESH LEMON JUICE, OLIVE OIL, SALT AND PEPPER IN A SMALL CUP.
DRIZZLE THE MIXTURE OVER THE ARUGULA (OR MIXED GREENS) AND LIGHTLY TOSS TO COAT.
DIVIDE THE HERBS AMONG SIX SERVING BOWLS AND TOP WITH THE COOKED PATTIES. DECORATE WITH FRESH CHIVES AND SERVE IMMEDIATELY WITH THE REMAINING DRESSING.

VEGAN MOUSSAKA

PREPARATION TIME 30 MINUTES
COOKING TIME 2 HOURS
SERVES: 12

INGREDIENTS:
5 LARGE RUSSET POTATOES, PEELED AND CUT INTO CHUNKS (3½LBS)
4 CLOVES GARLIC, PEELED
¼ CUP, PLUS 2 TBSP OLIVE OIL, DIVIDED
1 LARGE ONION, CHOPPED (1½ CUPS)
3 TBSP DRIED OREGANO
2 15OZ (430G) CANS CHOPPED TOMATOES
⅔ CUP GREEN LENTILS
1 BAY LEAF
1 CINNAMON STICK
2 MEDIUM EGGPLANTS, SLICED
2 SMALL ZUCCHINI, SLICED
3 TOMATOES, THINLY SLICED
SALT, TO TASTE
GROUND BLACK PEPPER, TO TASTE

DIRECTIONS:
1. PLACE THE PEELED POTATOES AND GARLIC IN A LARGE POT OF BOILING SALTED WATER AND COOK FOR 10 MINUTES, OR UNTIL TENDER. DRAIN, RESERVING THE COOKING LIQUID.
2. MASH THE POTATOES AND GARLIC, ADDING ¼ CUP OLIVE OIL AND 2 CUPS OF THE RESERVED LIQUID. SEASON THE PUREE WITH SALT AND PEPPER.
3. ADD 2 TABLESPOONS OF OLIVE OIL TO A LARGE GRIDDLE AND SET OVER A MODERATE HEAT.
4. STIR IN THE ONION AND OREGANO, AND SAUTÉ FOR 4-5 MINUTES, UNTIL GOLDEN AND TRANSLUCENT.

5. STIR IN THE LENTILS, TOMATOES, CINNAMON STICK AND BAY LEAF, AND POUR IN 3 CUPS OF THE RESERVED POTATO COOKING LIQUID. REDUCE THE HEAT AND SIMMER, COVERED, FOR ABOUT 40 MINUTES UNTIL THE LENTILS HAVE SOFTENED.

6. DISCARD THE CINNAMON STICK AND BAY LEAF. TRANSFER THE LENTIL MIXTURE TO A FOOD PROCESSOR AND PULSE UNTIL CHUNKY. SEASON THE PUREE WITH SALT AND PEPPER.

7. LINE A BAKING DISH WITH A PAPER TOWEL. ARRANGE THE EGGPLANT SLICES ON IT, SEASON WITH SALT AND LET IT SIT FOR 25-30 MINUTES. THEN SLIGHTLY RINSE AND DRAIN.

8. PREHEAT OVEN TO 350°F (170°C). OIL A DEEP BAKING DISH WITH COOKING SPRAY.

9. PLACE 1½ CUPS OF THE LENTIL MIXTURE INTO THE PREPARED DISH. IN AN EVEN LAYER ARRANGE THE EGGPLANT SLICES, ZUCCHINI AND TOP WITH TOMATOES. ADD A FURTHER 2 CUPS OF THE LENTIL MIXTURE ON TOP. TOP WITH HALF OF THE MASHED POTATOES, THEN PLACE THE REMAINING EGGPLANT SLICES, LAID OVER BY THE REMAINING LENTIL MIXTURE.

10. FINALLY, TOP WITH THE REMAINING POTATOES AND BAKE IN THE OVEN FOR 1½ HOURS, OR UNTIL GOLDEN BROWN.

Greek Style Hummus

TRADITIONAL HUMMUS IS A TASTY CHICKPEA DIP THAT IS WELL KNOWN IN GREECE, AS WELL AS ALL OVER THE WORLD. THIS IS A QUICK AND SIMPLE RECIPE OF GREEK-STYLE HUMMUS. ALTHOUGH THIS RECIPE CALLS FOR GARBANZO BEANS, TAHINI, LEMON AND GARLIC AS THE MAIN INGREDIENTS, YOU CAN ALSO ADD RED PEPPER FLAKES, BELL PEPPERS AND PINE NUTS. ENJOY WITH CRISPY PITA BREAD.

PREPARATION TIMES 10 MINUTES
COOKING TIME 0 MINUTES
SERVES: 2-4

INGREDIENTS:
1-2 CLOVES GARLIC, PRESSED

19 OZ (530G) CAN GARBANZO BEANS (RESERVE SOME LIQUID)
4 TBSP LEMON JUICE
2 TBSP TAHINI
1 TSP SALT
2 TBSP OLIVE OIL
GROUND BLACK PEPPER, TO TASTE

DIRECTIONS:
1. PLACE THE GARBANZO BEANS (INCLUDING GARBANZO LIQUID), TAHINI, GARLIC, OLIVE OIL, LEMON JUICE, SALT AND GROUND BLACK PEPPER IN A BLENDER AND PROCESS UNTIL SMOOTH. IF YOU GET A VERY THICK MIXTURE, ADD MORE BEAN LIQUID.
2. PLACE THE HUMMUS IN A SERVING BOWL, OR ADD TO THE SIDE OF A DINNER PLATE, DRIZZLE WITH A LITTLE OLIVE OIL AND SERVE.

Eggplant Purée with Walnuts

THE COMBINATION OF EGGPLANT AND SPINACH IS DELICIOUS. THIS HEALTHY DISH CAN BE SERVED EITHER AS A SIDE DISH OR AS A MAIN COURSE.

PREPARATION TIME 10 MINUTES
COOKING TIME 25 MINUTES
SERVES: 2

INGREDIENTS:
2 LARGE EGGPLANTS
2 - 4 GARLIC CLOVES, PEELED AND MINCED
½ CUP SHELLED WALNUTS, COARSELY CHOPPED
½ CUP EXTRA-VIRGIN OLIVE OIL
2 TBSP STRAINED FRESH LEMON JUICE
1 - 2 TBSP RED WINE VINEGAR
SALT, TO TASTE
½ -1 TSP SUGAR (OPTIONAL)

DIRECTIONS:
1. PREHEAT OVEN TO 450°F (220°C).
2. THOROUGHLY WASH THE EGGPLANTS AND DRAIN. USING A FORK, PIERCE THE EGGPLANTS IN SEVERAL PLACES.
3. PLACE THE EGGPLANTS ON AN UNGREASED BAKING DISH AND PLACE IN THE OVEN. BAKE FOR 20- 25 MINUTES, TURNING 1-2 TIMES, UNTIL THE SKIN IS SHRIVELED. WITHDRAW FROM THE OVEN AND LET THEM COOL FOR 5 MINUTES.
4. MEANWHILE, PLACE THE WALNUTS, GARLIC AND 2 TABLESPOONS OF THE OLIVE OIL IN A BLENDER AND PROCESS UNTIL THE MIXTURE RESEMBLES A PASTE.
5. REMOVE THE STEMS AND HALVE THE EGGPLANTS LENGTHWISE. SCRAPE OUT THE PULP WITH A SPOON, REMOVING THE SEEDS.

PLACE THE EGGPLANT IN A BLENDER AND PULSE FOR A SHORT TIME.

6. ADD THE VINEGAR, LEMON JUICE AND REMAINING OLIVE OIL, AND PROCESS UNTIL WELL BLENDED. SEASON WITH SALT TO TASTE, AND ENJOY. YOU MAY ADD A SMALL AMOUNT OF SUGAR AS EGGPLANTS CAN SOMETIMES HAVE A TRACE OF BITTERNESS.

GREEK FAVA
FAVA IS AN AUTHENTIC GREEK DISH MADE OF SPLIT PEAS. IT MAKES A PERFECT SIDE DISH OR APPETIZER.

PREPARATION TIMES 0 MINUTES
COOKING TIME 1 HOUR
SERVES: 4 - 6

INGREDIENTS:
1 CUP OF SANTORINI FAVA (OR YELLOW SPLIT PEAS)
1 MEDIUM-LARGE RED ONION, CHOPPED
2 TBSP OLIVE OIL
½ TSP SEA SALT

GARNISH
EXTRA VIRGIN OLIVE OIL
FRESHLY SQUEEZED LEMON JUICE
THINLY SLICED SPRING ONIONS
CAPERS

DIRECTIONS:
1. THOROUGHLY WASH THE FAVA AND PLACE IN A LARGE SAUCEPAN.
2. POUR IN ENOUGH WATER TO COVER, AND BRING TO A BOIL OVER MEDIUM-HIGH HEAT. WHEN A FROTH FORMS ON THE SURFACE OF THE WATER, POUR OFF THE WATER, RINSE THE FAVA AND RETURN BACK TO THE SAUCEPAN, ADDING 2½ CUPS OF WATER.
3. BRING THE WATER BACK TO THE BOIL. ONCE IT BEGINS TO BOIL, SLOW DOWN THE HEAT AND LET IT SIMMER FOR 40-50 MINUTES. YOU MAY NEED TO ADD MORE WATER IF YOU SEE THAT THE FAVA BEGINS TO DRY OUT. WHEN THE FAVA IS TENDER, REMOVE FROM THE HEAT AND LET THEM COOL.
4. PLACE THE FAVA IN A FOOD PROCESSOR OR BLENDER, AND PULSE UNTIL SMOOTH AND

CREAMY.
5. LADLE THE DISH INTO SMALL PLATES, DRIZZLE WITH LEMON JUICE AND OLIVE OIL, AND GARNISH WITH CHOPPED SPRING ONIONS AND CAPERS BEFORE SERVING.

Briam (Greek potato and zucchini bake)

BRIAM IS A TRADITIONAL GREEK POTATO-BASED BAKE, FLAVORED WITH OLIVE OIL AND FRESH PARSLEY. WARM OR COOL IT IS ABSOLUTELY DELICIOUS.

PREPARATION TIME 15 MINUTES
COOKING TIME 1 HR 30 MINUTES
SERVES: 4

INGREDIENTS;
2.2.2 LBS. (1KG) POTATOES, PEELED AND SLICED INTO ROUNDS
4 LARGE ZUCCHINIS, SLICED INTO ROUNDS
4 MEDIUM RED ONIONS, SLICED INTO ROUNDS
½ CUP (125ML) OLIVE OIL
6 FRESH PLUM TOMATOES, PUREED
2 TABLESPOONS FRESH PARSLEY, CHOPPED
SEA SALT, TO TASTE
GROUND BLACK PEPPER, TO TASTE

DIRECTIONS:
1. PREHEAT THE OVEN TO 390°F (200°C).
2. PLACE THE ZUCCHINI ROUNDS, POTATOES ROUNDS AND RED ONIONS IN A LARGE RIMMED BAKING DISH. TOP WITH THE PUREED TOMATOES, DRIZZLE WITH OLIVE OIL, AND SEASON WITH SALT, FRESHLY GROUND PEPPER AND PARSLEY.
3. GENTLY MIX THE VEGETABLES TO COAT EVENLY. ADD ABOUT ½ CUP OF WATER TO THE DISH AND TRANSFER TO THE OVEN.
4. BAKE THE MIXTURE FOR 90 MINUTES; STIRRING OCCASIONALLY AND ALSO ADDING A LITTLE MORE WATER IF NECESSARY TO PREVENT FROM STICKING TO THE BOTTOM. REMOVE THE DISH FROM THE OVEN, TASTE AND ADJUST WITH SEASONING IF NEEDED. LET IT STAND FOR 10 MINUTES TO COOL BEFORE SERVING.

Rice-Stuffed Tomatoes

THIS WONDERFUL RECIPE WAS PROVIDED BY A FRIEND FROM GREECE. THESE STUFFED TOMATOES ARE WONDERFUL HOT OR COOL. YOU CAN ENJOY THIS DISH WITH A POTATO SALAD AND SALAD GREENS.

PREPARATION TIME 15 MINUTES
COOKING TIME 55 MINUTES
SERVES: 6

INGREDIENTS:
1 BAY LEAF
1 TSP OLIVE OIL
1 CUP WHITE RICE
1-1½ CUPS VEGETABLE STOCK
1¼ CUPS WHITE WINE
6 MEDIUM TOMATOES
¼ CUP GREEN ONIONS, CHOPPED
¼ CUP FRESH BASIL LEAVES, CHOPPED

DIRECTIONS:
1. CUT A SMALL SLICE OFF THE TOPS OF THE TOMATOES AND SET ASIDE.
2. GENTLY DISCARD THE SEEDS WITH A TEASPOON. THINLY CHOP THE PULP AND PLACE IN A POT. PUT THE HOLLOWED TOMATOES, CUT SIDE DOWN, IN A BAKING DISH.
3. ADD THE RICE TO THE POT AND COOK FOR A MINUTE OVER A MEDIUM-HIGH HEAT.
4. POUR IN ¼ CUP OF THE WINE, THE VEGETABLE STOCK, OLIVE OIL AND THE BAY LEAF, AND COOK. ONCE BOILING, REDUCE THE HEAT AND SIMMER, COVERED, FOR 20-25 MINUTES, UNTIL ALL THE LIQUID IS ABSORBED.
5. REMOVE THE BAY LEAF. TURN OFF THE HEAT AND LET THE RICE COOL FOR AT LEAST 10 MINUTES.
6. PREHEAT THE OVEN TO 350°F (180°C).
7. ADD THE GREEN ONIONS AND BASIL TO THE COOLED RICE AND STIR WELL TO COMBINE.
8. FILL THE TOMATOES WITH THE COOKED RICE MIXTURE. PLACE THE STUFFED TOMATOES

ON THE BAKING DISH AND PLACE THE CUT TOP ON EACH TOMATO. SLIGHTLY COVER THE PAN WITH ALUMINUM FOIL.

9. BAKE THE TOMATOES IN THE OVEN FOR 20 MINUTES.

10. REMOVE THE FOIL, DRIZZLE THE TOMATOES WITH THE REMAINING WINE, AND LET THEM BAKE FOR ANOTHER 10 MINUTES. LET THE DISH STAND FOR 5 MINUTES BEFORE SERVING.

Salads
Greek Bulgur Salad

FRESH CUCUMBER AND CHERRY TOMATOES GIVE THIS HEALTHY DISH A BEAUTIFUL COLOR - IT'S ALSO FULL OF FIBER AND VITAMIN C.

PREPARATION TIME 35 MINUTES
COOKING TIME 0 MINUTE
SERVES: 4

INGREDIENTS:
3 CUPS BOILING WATER
1 CUP BULGUR
2 TBSP FRESH LEMON JUICE
1 TBSP OLIVE OIL
1 SMALL GARLIC CLOVE, MINCED
½ TBSP SALT
⅛ TSP FRESHLY GROUND PEPPER
¾ CUP FRESH MINT, CHOPPED
2 CUPS CHERRY TOMATOES, HALVED
1 SMALL CUCUMBER, PEELED, SEEDED AND CUT
4 LARGE ROMAINE LETTUCE LEAVES

DIRECTIONS:
1. PLACE THE BULGUR IN A LARGE BOWL, POUR IN 3 CUPS OF BOILING WATER AND IT LET STAND UNTIL THE BULGUR IS TENDER, FOR ABOUT 30 MINUTES.
2. USING A FINE-MESH SIEVE, DRAIN THE BULGUR AND PLACE BACK INTO THE BOWL.
3. ADD THE CUCUMBER, TOMATOES AND CHOPPED MINT TO THE BULGUR. STIR WELL THEN ADD THE OLIVE OIL, LEMON JUICE AND GARLIC. SEASON WITH SALT AND PEPPER. MIX WELL TO COMBINE.
4. PLACE THE LETTUCE LEAVES ONTO SERVING PLATES. SPOON THE SALAD ONTO THE LETTUCE AND SERVE. THIS SALAD IS GREAT SERVED WITH TOASTED PITA BREAD.

VEGAN GREEK QUINOA SALAD

THIS IS A VERY SIMPLE AUTHENTIC GREEK DISH. ADD SOME FRESHLY SQUEEZED LEMON JUICE TO THIS SALAD TO COMPLETE THE TASTE.

PREPARATION TIME 10 MINUTES
COOKING TIME 25 MINUTES
SERVES: 8-10

INGREDIENTS:
1½ CUPS QUINOA
3 CUPS WATER
½ CUP KALAMATA OLIVES, CUT
⅓ CUP PINE NUTS
½ CUP FRESH BASIL, COARSELY CHOPPED
1 CUP FRESH SPINACH, COARSELY CHOPPED
½ CUP FRESH PARSLEY, CHOPPED
½ CUP FRESH CILANTRO, CHOPPED
⅓ CUP SCALLION
⅔ CUP RED ONION
1 CUP TOFU
⅔ CUP WHITE DISTILLED VINEGAR
1 LEMON JUICE AND ZEST
3 GARLIC CLOVES, GRATED
1 TBSP TAHINI

DIRECTIONS:
1. POUR 3 CUPS OF WATER INTO A LARGE POT AND BRING TO A BOIL OVER A HIGH HEAT.
2. ADD THE QUINOA, COVER AND SIMMER OVER A MEDIUM-HEAT UNTIL THE QUINOA IS COOKED THROUGH AND ALL THE LIQUID IS ABSORBED. REMOVE FROM THE HEAT, TRANSFER TO A BOWL AND LET IT COOL COMPLETELY.
3. CUT THE TOFU INTO SMALL CUBES AND PLACE IN A BOWL. ADD HALF OF THE LEMON ZEST AND JUICE, ⅓ CUP VINEGAR AND 1 GRATED GARLIC CLOVE. LET THIS STAND TO MARINATE

FOR ABOUT 20 MINUTES.

4. IN A LARGE SALAD BOWL, COMBINE THE CHOPPED PARSLEY, BASIL, RED ONION, SCALLIONS AND CILANTRO. ADD THE COARSELY CHOPPED SPINACH AND THE CUT KALAMATA OLIVES.

5. IN A SMALL BOWL, MIX TOGETHER THE REMAINING LEMON JUICE AND ZEST, TAHINI, RESERVED VINEGAR AND GARLIC, AND SET ASIDE.

6. ADD THE MARINATED TOFU (WITH THE MARINADE) INTO THE BOWL OF CHOPPED HERBS AND VEGETABLES. STIR IN THE COOLED QUINOA AND POUR THE PREPARED DRESSING OVER THE SALAD, TOSS TO COMBINE.

7. SPRINKLE WITH CHOPPED PINE NUTS AND ENJOY.

Traditional Greek Potato Salad (Patatosalata)

THIS DISH IS A SIMPLE AND HEALTHY COMBINATION OF INGREDIENTS. THE ADDITION OF THE CHOPPED OLIVES ADDS A LOVELY "BITE" TO THIS SALAD. ONCE YOU TRY THIS DISH YOU WILL BE EAGER TO ENJOY IT AS OFTEN AS POSSIBLE.

PREPARATION TIME 5 MINUTES
COOKING TIME 20 MINUTES
SERVES: 6

INGREDIENTS:
2LBS (907G) ROUND RED POTATOES
KOSHER SALT
FRESHLY GROUND BLACK PEPPER, TO TASTE
⅓ CUP EXTRA VIRGIN OLIVE OIL
3 TBSP WHITE WINE VINEGAR
1½ CUPS PITTED KALAMATA OLIVES, ROUGHLY CHOPPED
⅓ CUP RED ONION, FINELY CHOPPED
2 TBSP FLAT-LEAF PARSLEY, CHOPPED

DIRECTIONS:
1. PLACE THE POTATOES IN A LARGE POT AND COVER WITH WATER. ADD 1 TABLESPOON OF SALT AND SET OVER A MEDIUM-HIGH HEAT TO BOIL.
2. ONCE BOILING, REDUCE THE HEAT AND SIMMER FOR 12-15 MINUTES UNTIL THE POTATOES ARE TENDER. POUR OFF THE WATER AND COOL FOR 15 MINUTES.
3. CHOP THE POTATOES INTO ½ INCH CUBES AND TRANSFER TO A LARGE GLASS SALAD BOWL.
4. COMBINE THE VINEGAR, OLIVE OIL, ONION AND CHOPPED OLIVES IN A SMALL BOWL, AND SEASON WITH SALT AND PEPPER.
5. POUR THE DRESSING OVER THE CHOPPED

POTATOES, SPRINKLE WITH CHOPPED PARSLEY AND GENTLY MIX TO COMBINE. THIS SALAD IS PERFECT SERVED WARM OR AT ROOM TEMPERATURE.

CUCUMBER SALAD

THIS IS ANOTHER REFRESHING SALAD YOU CAN TRY FOR YOUR FAMILY. IT CONTAINS CUCUMBERS, ONIONS AND FRESH HERBS WHICH MAKES IT VERY HEALTHY AND PROVIDES YOU WITH LOTS OF VITAMINS.
PREPARATION TIME 5 MINUTES
COOKING TIME 0 MINUTE
SERVES: 6

INGREDIENTS:
1 TSP FRESH OREGANO, CHOPPED
½ CUP RED ONION, THINLY SLICED
2 TBSP FRESH DILL, CHOPPED
2 TBSP RED WINE VINEGAR
2 TBSP FRESH MINT, CHOPPED
1½LBS (680G) CUCUMBERS, HALVED AND SEEDED
3 TBSP EXTRA VIRGIN OLIVE OIL
KOSHER SALT, TO TASTE
FRESHLY GROUND BLACK PEPPER, TO TASTE
HANDFUL OF PARSLEY, CHOPPED

DIRECTIONS:
1. SEED THE CUCUMBERS AND CUT EACH CUCUMBER LENGTHWISE INTO 4 PIECES, THEN CHOP THE CUCUMBERS CROSSWISE INTO THIN SLICES. PLACE THE CUCUMBERS IN A LARGE BOWL.
2. ADD THE OREGANO, ONION, DILL, MINT AND VINEGAR. SEASON THE SALAD WITH SALT AND PEPPER, DRIZZLE WITH THE OLIVE OIL, AND MIX TO COMBINE THE FLAVORS.
3. SPRINKLE WITH CHOPPED PARSLEY AND ENJOY.

Cabbage Salad (Lahanosalata)

LAHANOSALATA IS A CLASSIC AND AUTHENTIC GREEK SALAD, MOSTLY PREPARED IN COLD WEATHERS. FENNEL AND CILANTRO SEEDS, AS WELL AS FRESH THYME LEAVES AND LEMON JUICE MAKE THIS SIMPLE SALAD HEALTHY AND FLAVORFUL.

PREPARATION TIME 15 MINUTES
COOKING TIME 0
SERVES: 6

INGREDIENTS:
1 MEDIUM FENNEL BULB, NO STEMS OR FRONDS
1 MEDIUM (2LBS/907G) HEAD OF CABBAGE
⅓ CUP OLIVE OIL
2 TBSP FRESHLY SQUEEZED LEMON JUICE
3 TBSP RED WINE VINEGAR
¼ CUP FRESH THYME LEAVES
1 TSP SALT
½ TSP FRESHLY GROUND PEPPER
2 TSP MUSTARD POWDER
2 TSP FENNEL SEEDS
2 TSP CILANTRO SEEDS
DIRECTIONS:

1. REMOVE THE CORE FROM THE CABBAGE AND CUT THE CABBAGE AND FENNEL BULB INTO VERY THIN STRIPS. PLACE THE FENNEL INTO A LARGE SALAD BOWL. USING YOUR FINGERS, BREAK UP THE CABBAGE TO SEPARATE THE THIN STRIPS, AND SET ASIDE.
2. GRIND THE FENNEL SEEDS AND CILANTRO SEEDS IN A MORTAR AND PESTLE UNTIL FINELY GROUND. TRANSFER TO A SMALL BOWL. ADD THE OLIVE OIL, MUSTARD POWDER, FRESHLY SQUEEZED LEMON JUICE AND OLIVE OIL, AND STIR WELL TO COMBINE.
3. ADD THE MIXTURE TO THE SLICED CABBAGE AND FENNEL, ADD THYME LEAVES AND MIX TO COAT.
4. LET THE SALAD STAND FOR 5-10 MINUTES SO ALL OF THE FLAVORS ARE COMBINED BEFORE SERVING.

GREEK ORZO SALAD WITH TOMATOES
THIS IS A WONDERFUL PASTA SALAD FULL OF SUMMER FLAVORS. IT IS QUICKLY PREPARED YET PROVIDES YOU WITH AN UNFORGETTABLE EXPERIENCE.

PREPARATION TIME 5 MINUTES
COOK TIME 10 MINUTES
SERVES: 4 – 6

INGREDIENTS:
1 CUP ORZO, UNCOOKED
½ CUP DILL, CHOPPED
3 TBSP EXTRA VIRGIN OLIVE OIL
1 TSP LEMON ZEST (GRATED)
2 CUPS CHERRY TOMATOES (HALVED)
¾ CUP BLACK OLIVES, PREFERABLY KALAMATA, PITTED AND HALVED
SALT, TO TASTE
GROUND BLACK PEPPER, TO TASTE

DIRECTIONS:
1. PLACE THE PASTA IN A POT OF BOILING SALTED WATER AND COOK UNTIL AL DENTE.
2. MEANWHILE, IN A LARGE SALAD BOWL, COMBINE THE TOMATOES, OLIVES, OIL, DILL AND GRATED LEMON ZEST, AND SEASON WITH ½ TEASPOON EACH OF SALT AND PEPPER.
3. LET THE MIXTURE SIT FOR 10-15 MINUTES.
4. DRAIN THE COOKED ORZO IN A COLANDER AND ADD TO THE BOWL WITH THE TOMATO MIXTURE. MIX WELL TO COAT.

Greek Couscous Salad with Avocado

THIS IS A VERY TASTY AND HEALTHY SALAD RECIPE WHICH CAN BE MADE IN A SHORT TIME. SO MAKE SURE YOU HAVE ALL THE INGREDIENTS ON HAND AND START EXPERIENCING!

PREPARATION TIME 20 MINUTES
COOKING TIME 5 MINUTES
SERVES: 4

INGREDIENTS:
1 CUP WATER
1 CUP COUSCOUS
1½ TBSP OLIVE OIL (GOOD QUALITY)
2 TBSP RED WINE VINEGAR
2 TBSP LEMON (FRESHLY SQUEEZED)
2 DASHES OF DRIED OREGANO
1 HANDFUL TOMATOES, CHOPPED
1 HANDFUL CUCUMBER, CHOPPED
2 SLICES PURPLE ONION, CHOPPED
½ AVOCADO, DICED
1 HANDFUL ARUGULA
SALT, TO TASTE
GROUND BLACK PEPPER, TO TASTE

DIRECTIONS:
1. ADD 1 CUP WATER TO A MEDIUM SAUCEPAN AND SET OVER HIGH HEAT. ONCE IT IS BOILING, STIR IN THE COUSCOUS AND THEN TURN OFF THE HEAT. LET THE COUSCOUS STAND FOR ABOUT 5 MINUTES, COVERED.
2. IN A SMALL CUP COMBINE TOGETHER THE VINEGAR, OLIVE OIL, OREGANO AND LEMON AND SET ASIDE.
3. PLACE THE CHOPPED CUCUMBER, TOMATOES AND ONION IN A MEDIUM SALAD BOWL. POUR THE DRESSING OVER THE

VEGETABLES. ADD THE COUSCOUS TO THE BOWL AND GENTLY MIX TO COMBINE.

4. ADD A HANDFUL OF ARUGULA TO A SERVING PLATE, FLAVOR WITH SALT AND DRIZZLE WITH OLIVE OIL, IF DESIRED. SPOON THE COUSCOUS SALAD ON THE PLATE. PLACE A PIECE OF AVOCADO ON TOP OF THE SALAD AND SERVE.

Greek Vegan Salad

THIS IS A FANTASTIC PLAIN SALAD RECIPE THAT FEATURES CLASSIC INGREDIENTS FOR A GREEK SALAD. IT IS QUICK AND EASY TO MAKE, AND VERY REFRESHING.

PREPARATION TIME 10 MINUTES
COOKING TIME 0 MINUTE
SERVES: 4

INGREDIENTS:
3 CUPS TOMATO, DICED
3 TBSP FRESH DILL, COARSELY CHOPPED
1 TBSP EXTRA VIRGIN OLIVE OIL
1 TBSP FRESH LEMON JUICE
1 TSP OREGANO, DRIED

¼ CUP FRESH PARSLEY, COARSELY CHOPPED
6 CUPS ROMAINE LETTUCE, SHREDDED
1 CUP RED ONION, THINLY SLICED
6 (6-INCH) WHOLE WHEAT PITAS, EACH CUT INTO 8 WEDGES
1 TBSP CAPERS
1 19OZ (540G) CAN OF CHICKPEAS, DRAINED AND RINSED
1 CUCUMBER, PEELED AND THINLY SLICED

DIRECTIONS:
1. IN A SMALL CUP MIX TOGETHER THE OLIVE OIL, FRESH DILL, PARSLEY AND OREGANO.
2. IN A LARGE SALAD BOWL COMBINE TOGETHER THE LETTUCE, DRAINED CHICKPEAS, RED ONION, CAPERS, , CUCUMBER AND TOMATOES.
3. POUR THE PREPARED DRESSING OVER THE SALAD, STIR WELL UNTIL BLENDED.
4. SERVE THE SALAD WITH PITA WEDGES.

Soups and stews

Greek Potato Stew

THIS IS A VERY SIMPLE, BUT A VERY TASTY GREEK DISH. THE KALAMATA OLIVES AND GARLIC PROVIDE IT WITH A WONDERFUL FLAVOR. SERVE WITH PLENTY OF GOOD BREAD TO MOP UP THE DELICIOUS JUICES.

PREPARATION TIME 25 MINUTES
COOKING TIME 30 MINUTES
SERVES: 6

INGREDIENTS:
2½LBS (1134G) POTATOES, PEELED AND CUBED
⅓ CUPS OLIVE OIL
2 CLOVES GARLIC, MINCED
¾ CUP WHOLE KALAMATA OLIVES, PITTED
1⅓ CUPS TOMATOES, CHOPPED
1 TSP DRIED OREGANO
SALT, TO TASTE
GROUND BLACK PEPPER, TO TASTE

DIRECTIONS:
1. ADD THE OLIVE OIL TO A LARGE FRYING PAN AND SET OVER A MODERATE HEAT.
2. STIR IN THE CUBED POTATOES AND GARLIC, AND SAUTÉ FOR A FEW MINUTES.
3. ADD THE OLIVES AND COOK FOR 3-4 MINUTES, STIRRING FREQUENTLY.
4. ADD THE CHOPPED TOMATOES AND OREGANO, REDUCE THE HEAT AND SIMMER, COVERED, FOR 25 MINUTES, OR UNTIL THE POTATOES ARE FORK-TENDER.
5. SEASON THE STEW WITH SALT AND PEPPER, AND SERVE IMMEDIATELY.

Fasolada

FASOLADA IS A TRADITIONAL GREEK DISH THAT IS A FLAVORFUL COMBINATION OF BEANS, TOMATOES, CARROTS AND VARIOUS HEALTHY SPICES. BEAN LOVERS WILL APPRECIATE THIS.

PREPARATION TIME 5 MINUTES
COOKING TIME 1 HR 5 MINUTES
SERVES: 4

INGREDIENTS:
1 CUP WHITE KIDNEY BEANS
1 ONION, THINLY SLICED
2 SMALL CARROTS, SLICED
1 STALK CELERY, CHOPPED
1 14.5OZ CAN DICED TOMATOES
1 TBSP TOMATO PASTE
1 TSP DRIED OREGANO
1 TSP DRIED THYME

½ CUP OLIVE OIL
2 TBSP FRESH PARSLEY, CHOPPED
SALT, TO TASTE
GROUND BLACK PEPPER, TO TASTE
DIRECTIONS:
1. SOAK THE BEANS IN COLD WATER AND LET THEM STAND OVERNIGHT. SLIGHTLY RINSE AND DRAIN IN A COLANDER.
2. TRANSFER THE BEANS TO A LARGE POT. COVER WITH WATER AND BRING TO A BOIL. AFTER 3-4 MINUTES POUR OFF THE BOILING WATER, ADD 3 CUPS FRESH COLD WATER AND SET OVER A MEDIUM-HIGH HEAT.
3. ONCE THE WATER RETURNS TO THE BOIL STIR IN THE CARROTS, TOMATOES, ONIONS, TOMATO PASTE, THYME, OLIVE OIL, OREGANO AND CELERY, AND SEASON WITH SALT AND PEPPER. LET THE DISH SIMMER OVER LOW HEAT FOR ABOUT AN HOUR UNTIL THE BEANS ARE TENDER. IN THE END, ADD THE CHOPPED PARSLEY, GIVE A STIR AND REMOVE THE SOUP FROM THE HEAT.

Cabbage Soup

THIS IS A GREAT TRADITIONAL DISH FOR COLD SEASONS IN GREECE THE ORDER OF ADDING THE VEGETABLES IS VERY IMPORTANT IN THIS RECIPE AS IT MAKES THIS DISH HEALTHIER AND MORE FLAVORFUL.

PREPARATION TIME 10 MINUTES
COOKING TIME 30 MINUTES
SERVES: 6
INGREDIENTS:
5 CUPS CHOPPED CABBAGE
⅓ CUP OLIVE OIL
½ CUP CHOPPED ONIONS
⅓ CUP CHOPPED GARLIC
2 CUPS CUBED POTATOES
1 CUP CHOPPED CARROTS
1 CUP CHOPPED ZUCCHINI
2 TBSP FRESHLY CHOPPED DILL
2 TSP DRIED CRUSHED THYME
1½ TBSP SALT
1½ TSP FRESHLY GROUND BLACK PEPPER
7 CUPS WATER
3 TBSP FRESHLY SQUEEZED LEMON JUICE
DIRECTIONS:
1. HEAT THE OLIVE OIL IN A LARGE SAUCEPAN OVER A MEDIUM-LOW HEAT. ADD THE ONIONS AND SAUTÉ UNTIL LIGHTLY GOLDEN AND TRANSLUCENT, ABOUT 3-4 MINUTES.
2. STIR IN THE GARLIC AND SAUTÉ FOR ANOTHER MINUTE, UNTIL JUST TENDER. ADD THE THYME, DILL AND SPRINKLE WITH SALT AND PEPPER. LET IT COOK FOR 2-3 MINUTES ON A LOW HEAT.
3. ADD THE CHOPPED CARROTS AND ZUCCHINI, STIR, AND COOK FOR 10-12 MINUTES.
4. STIR IN THE CABBAGE AND COOK FOR A

FURTHER 2-3 MINUTES, UNTIL THE CABBAGE IS ABOUT TO WILT. FOLD IN THE CUBED POTATOES, STIR UNTIL THEY ARE COATED WITH OLIVE OIL, AND COOK FOR 6-7 MINUTES.

5. POUR IN THE WATER, INCREASE THE HEAT TO MEDIUM-HIGH, AND BRING THE SOUP TO A BOIL. LET THE SOUP COOK FOR 15-18 MINUTES UNTIL THE POTATOES AND CARROTS HAVE SOFTENED.

6. FINALLY, DRIZZLE THE SOUP WITH LEMON JUICE AND ENJOY. THIS SOUP IS PERFECT SERVED WITH A PIECE OF CRUSTY BREAD.

Manestra (Orzo Soup)

MANESTRA IS AN AUTHENTIC GREEK DISH THAT'S PERFECT FOR COLD WINTER DAYS. THE FLAVOR IS WONDERFUL AND IT IS SO SIMPLE TO PREPARE THAT YOU WILL BE AMAZED AT HOW SUCH A FILLING DISH CAN BE SO QUICK AND EASY TO MAKE.

PREPARATION TIME 5 MINUTES
COOKING TIME 30 MINUTES
SERVES: 4

INGREDIENTS:
2 CUPS WHOLE, PEELED TOMATOES
1½ CUPS ORZO
⅓ CUP OLIVE OIL
1 CUP ONION, CHOPPED
2 TBSP DRIED, CRUSHED GREEK OREGANO
1 TSP SALT
1 TSP FRESHLY GROUND PEPPER
4 CUPS WATER

DIRECTIONS:
1. ADD THE OLIVE OIL TO A MEDIUM SAUCEPAN AND SET OVER A MEDIUM HEAT. ADD THE ONIONS AND COOK FOR 3-4 MINUTES, UNTIL LIGHTLY GOLDEN AND TENDER.
2. STIR IN THE OREGANO, TOMATOES, ORZO AND SEASON WITH SALT AND PEPPER. COOK FOR ABOUT 5-6 MINUTES OVER A LOW HEAT.
3. ADD THE WATER, COVER, AND COOK FOR 20-25 MINUTES. STIR FREQUENTLY TO AVOID STICKING TO THE BOTTOM OF THE PAN. THIS SOUP IS PERFECT SERVED WITH CRUSTY BREAD.

Spicy Greek Pumpkin Soup

THIS IS A VERY TASTY AND HEALTHY SOUP, FULL OF SPICES AND IT IS VERY SIMPLE TO PREPARE. SURE, YOUR KIDS WILL ADORE IT.
PREPARATION TIME 5 MINUTES
COOKING TIME 40 MINUTES
SERVES: 4

INGREDIENTS:
2LBS (907G) PUMPKIN, PEELED AND SEEDED
2 TSP EXTRA VIRGIN OLIVE OIL
2 LEEKS, TRIMMED AND SLICED
1 GARLIC CLOVE, CRUSHED
1 TSP GINGER, GROUND
1 TSP CUMIN, GROUND
3 CUPS VEGETABLE STOCK OR WATER
SALT, TO TASTE
BLACK PEPPER, TO TASTE
CILANTRO LEAF, CHOPPED

DIRECTIONS:
1. PEEL THE PUMPKIN AND CUT INTO COARSE PIECES. ADD THE OIL TO A LARGE SAUCEPAN AND SET OVER A MEDIUM HEAT.

2. ADD THE LEEKS AND GARLIC, AND COOK UNTIL TENDER.
3. STIR IN THE CUMIN AND GINGER, AND COOK FOR A FURTHER MINUTE. ADD THE PUMPKIN PIECES, POUR IN THE STOCK/WATER, SPRINKLE WITH SALT AND PEPPER, AND COOK OVER A MODERATE HEAT.
4. ONCE BOILING, REDUCE THE HEAT TO LOW AND SIMMER FOR 25-30 MINUTES, UNTIL THE PUMPKIN HAS SOFTENED.
5. TRANSFER THE SOUP TO A BLENDER AND PULSE UNTIL PUREED.
6. RETURN THE SOUP BACK TO THE SAUCEPAN AND HEAT FOR 1-2 MINUTES. DIVIDE THE SOUP AMONG SERVING BOWLS, SPRINKLE WITH FRESHLY CHOPPED CILANTRO, AND SERVE IMMEDIATELY.

Greek Stew with Green Beans and Potato

THIS IS AN EASY AND TASTY DISH WHICH IS FULL OF HEALTHY VEGETABLES AND HERBS. THE ADDITION OF CHOPPED ONIONS GIVES IT A NICE CRUNCH.

PREPARATION 5 MINUTES
COOKING TIME 30 MINUTES
SERVES: 10
INGREDIENTS:
1 ONION, CHOPPED
1 TBSP OLIVE OIL
1LB GREEN BEANS, CUT
1 28OZ CAN WHOLE PLUM TOMATOES, WITH JUICE
2 ZUCCHINIS, CUT INTO HALF MOONS
1 LARGE POTATO, PEELED AND CUT INTO CUBES
¼ CUP WHITE WINE
GARLIC, CAYENNE, OREGANO AND THYME, TO TASTE

SALT, TO TASTE
BLACK PEPPER, TO TASTE
FRESHLY CHOPPED PARSLEY

DIRECTIONS:
1. ADD THE OLIVE OIL TO A LARGE SAUCEPAN AND SET OVER A MEDIUM HEAT. ADD THE ONION AND COOK FOR 3-4 MINUTES, UNTIL LIGHTLY GOLDEN AND TENDER.
2. ADD THE GREEN BEANS, STIR, AND COOK FOR ABOUT 5 MINUTES. STIR IN THE CHOPPED ZUCCHINI, POTATO, TOMATOES AND GARLIC, WHITE WINE AND SEASON WITH THE GARLIC, CAYENNE, OREGANO, THYME, SALT AND PEPPER.
3. ONCE THE STEW BEGINS TO BOIL, REDUCE THE HEAT AND SIMMER, COVERED, FOR ABOUT 20 MINUTES UNTIL THE POTATOES HAVE SOFTENED.
4. LADLE THE STEW INTO A SERVING BOWL, SPRINKLE WITH FRESH PARSLEY AND SERVE WITH TOASTED BREAD.

Fasolakia (Green Bean Stew)

THIS IS NOT A SIMPLE RECIPE TO MAKE, BUT IT IS DEFINITELY A WORTHWHILE RECIPE. FASOLAKIA IS ONE OF THE MASTERPIECES OF THE GREEK CUISINE. IT IS THE PERFECT DISH TO IMPRESS YOUR GUESTS.

PREPARATION TIME 15 MINUTES
COOKING TIME 1 HR 15 MINUTES
SERVES: 6 - 8
INGREDIENTS:
2.2LBS (1KG) FRESH GREEN BEANS, TRIMMED
½ CUP OLIVE OIL
2 ONIONS, PEELED AND GRATED
4 CLOVES OF GARLIC, MINCED
8 ROMA TOMATOES, PEELED AND CHOPPED
2 TBSP FRESH PARSLEY, FINELY CHOPPED
½ CUP WATER
SALT, TO TASTE
BLACK PEPPER, TO TASTE
DIRECTIONS:
1. WASH THE BEANS UNDER COLD WATER. DRAIN AND REMOVE THE ENDS.
2. ADD THE OLIVE OIL TO A LARGE GRIDDLE AND SET OVER A MODERATE HEAT. ADD THE ONIONS AND GARLIC, AND SAUTÉ FOR 3-4 MINUTES, UNTIL LIGHTLY GOLDEN AND FRAGRANT.
3. ADD THE TRIMMED BEANS AND STIR FRY FOR 1-2 MINUTES. STIR IN THE TOMATOES, ADD THE WATER AND SEASON WITH SALT AND PEPPER.
4. PUT THE LID ON AND SIMMER OVER A LOW HEAT FOR 60-80 MINUTES, UNTIL THE BEANS ARE CRISP-TENDER.
5. FINALLY, STIR IN THE PARSLEY, AND SIMMER FOR A FURTHER 5-8 MINUTES, UNCOVERED,

UNTIL THE TOMATO SAUCE HAS THICKENED.
6. SERVE IMMEDIATELY.

Greek Chickpeas with Spinach

The combination of spinach and lemon juice is fantastic. Give a try and this stew will become your favorite.

PREPARATION TIME 20 MINUTES
COOKING TIME 1HR 20 MINUTES
SERVES: 6 - 8

INGREDIENTS:
9OZ (250G) CHICKPEAS
2.2LBS (1KG) FRESH SPINACH, ROUGHLY CHOPPED
1 ONION WHOLE
1 LARGE RED PEPPER, DICED
2 CHILI PEPPERS, FINELY CHOPPED
2 TOMATOES, SKINNED AND DICED
1 BUNCH SPRING ONIONS, FINELY CHOPPED
4 TBSP WILD FENNEL, FINELY CHOPPED
2 TBSP PARSLEY, CHOPPED
1 TSP CUMIN POWDER
1 TSP PAPRIKA
1 TBSP LEMON JUICE
½ CUP OLIVE OIL
SALT, TO TASTE
GROUND BLACK PEPPER, TO TASTE

DIRECTIONS:
1. PLACE THE CHICKPEAS IN A POT OF COLD WATER AND LET THEM STAND OVERNIGHT.
2. ADD A WHOLE ONION TO THE CHICKPEAS AND BRING TO THE BOIL. ONCE BOILING POUR OFF THE WATER, ADD FRESH BOILING WATER, AND COOK FOR ABOUT AN HOUR OR MORE, UNTIL THE CHICKPEAS HAVE SOFTENED.
3. TRANSFER TO A COLANDER, DRAIN AND SET ASIDE.
4. ADD THE OIL TO A LARGE SAUCEPAN AND SET OVER A MEDIUM-HIGH HEAT. ADD THE RED

PEPPER, SPRING ONIONS AND CHILI PEPPERS, AND COOK FOR 3-4 MINUTES.

5. STIR IN THE TOMATOES AND ADD THE PAPRIKA AND CUMIN.

6. COVER THE SAUCEPAN AND SIMMER FOR 4-5 MINUTES. STIR IN THE CHICKPEAS, SPINACH AND FENNEL, SEASON WITH SALT, STIR, AND SIMMER FOR 10-12 MINUTES, UNCOVERED.

7. STIR IN THE LEMON JUICE, SPRINKLE WITH PEPPER AND CHOPPED PARSLEY. LET THE DISH STAND FOR 5 MINUTES BEFORE SERVING.

Pureed Split Pea Soup

MOST OF US USUALLY HAVE A HARD TIME PERSUADING OUR KIDS TO EAT A SPOON OF SOUP. BE SURE, KIDS WILL ASK YOU FOR MORE OF THIS DELICIOUS AND HEALTHY SOUP.

PREPARATION TIME 10 MINUTES
COOKING TIME 1 HR 20 MINUTES
SERVES: 6 - 8

INGREDIENTS:
1LB (454G) SPLIT PEAS

2 LARGE VEGETABLE BOUILLON CUBES
1 LARGE CARROT, CHOPPED
2 STALKS OF CELERY WITH LEAVES, CHOPPED
½ BUNCH OF FRESH PARSLEY, CHOPPED
1 BAY LEAF
⅓ CUP OF OLIVE OIL
SEA SALT, TO TASTE
FRESHLY GROUND PEPPER, TO TASTE
1 TSP DRIED THYME
7-8 CUPS OF WATER

DIRECTIONS:
1. RINSE THE PEAS UNDER COLD WATER AND DRAIN IN A COLANDER. TRANSFER TO A LARGE POT OF COLD WATER AND LET THE PEAS STAND FOR 6-8 HOURS, OR OVERNIGHT.
2. POUR OFF THE WATER AND SLIGHTLY RINSE THE PEAS. ADD THE BOUILLON CUBES, OLIVE OIL, CHOPPED CARROTS, CHOPPED PARSLEY, THYME, BAY LEAF AND CELERY TO THE POT. POUR IN THE WATER, SEASON WITH SALT AND PEPPER, AND BRING THE POT TO A BOIL OVER A MEDIUM–HIGH HEAT.
3. REDUCE THE HEAT, COVER AND SIMMER FOR ABOUT 2 HOURS, STIRRING OCCASIONALLY TO AVOID ANY STICKING TO THE BOTTOM OF THE POT. TASTE THE SOUP AND WHEN YOU SEE THAT THE PEAS ARE TENDER, AND THE SOUP HAS THICKENED ENOUGH, REMOVE THE POT FROM THE HEAT. MAKE SURE THAT YOU DO NOT OVERCOOK THE SOUP.
4. LET THE SOUP COOL FOR 8-10 MINUTES. DISCARD THE BAY LEAF.
5. TRANSFER THE SOUP TO A BLENDER AND PULSE UNTIL PUREED. LADLE THE SOUP INTO SERVING BOWLS AND ENJOY!

Greek Mains
Orzo with Zucchini

THE THREE MOST POPULAR FLAVORS OF GREECE ARE INCORPORATED INTO THIS RECIPE: GARLIC, OREGANO AND LEMON. COMBINE THESE WITH THE ORZO, SQUASH AND A SPLASH OF WHITE WINE AND I PROMISE YOU WILL CREATE AN UNFORGETTABLE EXPERIENCE.

PREPARATION TIME 10 MINUTES
COOKING TIME 25 MINUTES
SERVES: 6

INGREDIENTS:
2 CUPS ORZO, UNCOOKED
3-4 MEDIUM ZUCCHINI OR YELLOW SQUASH
½ SWEET ONION, CHOPPED
½ CUP OLIVE OIL
½ CUP WHITE WINE
1 TSP SALT
1 TSP FRESHLY GROUND PEPPER
2 TBSP DRIED OREGANO
2 TBSP FRESHLY SQUEEZED LEMON JUICE
4 CUPS VEGETABLE STOCK
2 CUPS WATER

DIRECTIONS:
1. ADD 2 CUPS OF WATER AND 4 CUPS OF VEGETABLE STOCK TO A LARGE POT AND SET OVER A MEDIUM-HIGH HEAT. STIR IN THE ORZO AND LET IT COOK FOR ABOUT 10 MINUTES, UNTIL JUST TENDER.
2. DRAIN WELL, DRIZZLE WITH 1 TEASPOON OF OLIVE OIL AND SET ASIDE.
3. ADD THE REMAINING OLIVE OIL TO A MEDIUM SKILLET AND SET OVER A LOW HEAT. ADD THE CHOPPED ONIONS, ZUCCHINI AND

COOK, STIRRING FREQUENTLY, UNTIL THE ONIONS ARE SLIGHTLY GOLDEN AND TRANSLUCENT.

4. ADD THE WHITE WINE AND OREGANO, AND SPRINKLE WITH SALT AND GROUND PEPPER. STIR WELL TO COMBINE. CONTINUE COOKING FOR AN ADDITIONAL 10 MINUTES.

5. STIR IN THE ORZO. AFTER 1-2 MINUTES ADD THE LEMON JUICE, COVER AND COOK FOR A FURTHER 10 MINUTES.

6. SERVE THE ORZO DISH IMMEDIATELY, OR AT ROOM TEMPERATURE.

SPANAKORIZO (SPINACH AND RICE)

SPINACH IS A GREAT PROPHYLACTIC METHOD FOR THE PREVENTION OF CANCER, CARDIOVASCULAR DEFICIENCY AND THE DEGENERATION OF THE IMMUNE AND NEUROLOGICAL SYSTEMS. THIS DISH CAN EASILY BE INCORPORATED INTO YOUR HEALTHY LIFESTYLE AND, ONCE YOU TRY IT, YOU WILL TURN TO IT AGAIN AND AGAIN.

PREPARATION 5 MINUTES
COOKING TIME 45
SERVES: 4 - 6

INGREDIENTS:
2-3LBS FRESH SPINACH, RINSED AND CHOPPED
¼ CUP OLIVE OIL
1 CUP ONION, CHOPPED
⅓ CUP GARLIC, CHOPPED
¼ CUP FRESHLY CHOPPED DILL OR FRESHLY CHOPPED MINT
1 TABLESPOON DRIED GREEK OREGANO
1 CUP WHITE RICE (MEDIUM GRAIN)
3 CUPS WATER
1½ TSP SALT, TO TASTE
1 TSP FRESHLY GROUND BLACK PEPPER, TO TASTE
½ CUP TOMATO PASTE DISSOLVED IN ½ CUP WARM WATER (OPTIONAL)

DIRECTIONS:
1. HEAT THE OLIVE OIL IN A LARGE NONSTICK SAUCEPAN OVER A LOW HEAT. ADD THE ONIONS AND GARLIC, AND COOK FOR A FEW MINUTES UNTIL TENDER.
2. STIR IN THE OREGANO AND DILL/MINT, AND SEASON WITH SALT AND PEPPER. STIR WITH A WOODEN SPATULA TO COMBINE WELL.
3. DISSOLVE THE TOMATO PASTE IN ½ CUP OF WARM WATER AND ADD TO THE POT.
4. STIR IN THE RICE AND CONTINUE COOKING

FOR A FURTHER 5 MINUTES. STIR OCCASIONALLY TO PREVENT STICKING ON THE BOTTOM. IF YOU NOTICE THE RICE BEGINS TO STICK TO THE BOTTOM SLIGHTLY REDUCE THE HEAT.

5. ADD THE SPINACH, POUR IN 3 CUPS OF WATER, STIR, AND BRING THE MIXTURE TO A BOIL.

6. ONCE IT IS BOILING, REDUCE THE HEAT AND SIMMER, COVERED, FOR ABOUT 30 MINUTES, OR UNTIL THE RICE IS TENDER.

7. REMOVE THE SAUCEPAN FROM THE HEAT AND LET IT STAND, COVERED, FOR 10-15 MINUTES BEFORE SERVING.

Greek Vegetables

THIS IS A WONDERFUL WAY TO USE FRESH TOMATOES AND CUCUMBERS FROM YOUR GARDEN. THIS DISH IS A GREAT COMBINATION OF VEGETABLE FLAVORS, AND IT CONTAINS A WHOLE ARSENAL OF VITAMINS AND NUTRIENTS.

PREPARATION TIME 10 MINUTES
COOKING TIME 35 MINUTES
SERVES: 6

INGREDIENTS:
1 CLOVE GARLIC, MINCED
1 TSP DRIED OREGANO
SALT, TO TASTE
GROUND BLACK PEPPER, TO TASTE
6 TBSP EXTRA VIRGIN OLIVE OIL
8 RED POTATOES, CUT INTO QUARTERS
10 CRIMINI MUSHROOMS, QUARTERED
1 LARGE ZUCCHINI, CUT IN HALF LENGTHWISE, THEN CUT INTO MOONS

DIRECTIONS:
1. HEAT THE OLIVE OIL IN A LARGE SKILLET OVER A MEDIUM HEAT. ADD THE OREGANO, GARLIC, SALT AND GROUND BLACK PEPPER, AND SAUTÉ FOR A MINUTE UNTIL FRAGRANT.
2. STIR IN THE MUSHROOMS, POTATOES AND ZUCCHINI.
3. COVER THE SKILLET AND SAUTÉ THE VEGETABLES OVER A MEDIUM TO HIGH HEAT FOR 5-6 MINUTES.
4. UNCOVER, REDUCE THE HEAT TO MEDIUM-LOW, AND COOK, STIRRING FREQUENTLY, UNTIL THE POTATOES HAVE SOFTENED AND ARE SLIGHTLY GOLDEN, FOR ABOUT 12-15 MINUTES.

Dolmades (Stuffed Grape Leaves)

PREPARATION TIME 15 MINUTES 50-60 MINUTES
COOKING TIME 45 MINUTES
MAKES: 50 DOLMADES

INGREDIENTS:
1 16OZ (454G) BOTTLE OF GRAPE LEAVES, DRAINED AND UNROLLED
¾ CUP EXTRA-VIRGIN OLIVE OIL
3 CLOVES GARLIC, MINCED
2 SCALLIONS, MINCED
1 LARGE YELLOW ONION, MINCED
⅔ CUP LONG-GRAIN RICE
KOSHER SALT, TO TASTE
FRESHLY GROUND BLACK PEPPER, TO TASTE
3 TBSP FRESH DILL, MINCED
½ CUP FRESH LEMON JUICE

DIRECTIONS:
1. PLACE THE GRAPE LEAVES IN A 5-QT. POT OF BOILING WATER AND COOK FOR 1-2 MINUTES OVER A MODERATE HEAT. GENTLY DRAIN, STEM

THE LEAVES AND SET ASIDE.
2. POUR ½ CUP OIL INTO A LARGE FRYING PAN AND SET OVER A MEDIUM-HIGH HEAT.
3. ADD THE ONIONS, SCALLIONS AND GARLIC, AND COOK UNTIL TENDER, STIRRING FREQUENTLY, FOR ABOUT 3-5 MINUTES. STIR IN THE RICE AND STIR-FRY FOR 2-3 MINUTES UNTIL TOASTED.
4. POUR IN 1¾ CUPS OF WATER, SPRINKLE WITH SALT AND PEPPER, AND COOK COVERED, STIRRING FROM TIME TO TIME, FOR A FURTHER 15 MINUTES, OR UNTIL ALL THE LIQUID HAS BEEN ABSORBED.
5. ADD THE DILL, STIR, AND REMOVE THE RICE FROM THE HEAT.
6. PLACE 4-5 GRAPE LEAVES ON THE BOTTOM OF THE POT.
7. TO START ROLLING THE DOLMADES: PLACE 2 TEASPOONS OF THE RICE MIXTURE IN THE CENTER OF EACH LEAF AND FOLD THE LEAF OVER THE RICE. THEN FOLD THE LEFT AND RIGHT EDGES OVER THE TOP, AND GENTLY ROLL TO GET A SMALL CYLINDER. PLACE THE FOLDED DOLMADES IN THE POT, SEAM SIDE DOWN. REPEAT THIS UNTIL ALL THE FILLING AND GRAPE LEAVES HAVE BEEN USED.
8. IN A SMALL BOWL, MIX TOGETHER THE LEMON JUICE, REMAINING OIL AND 1 CUP OF WATER, AND POUR OVER THE STUFFED LEAVES. PUT A SMALL PLATE OVER THE DOLMADES TO ENSURE THEY REMAIN SUBMERGED, AND PUT THE POT OVER A MEDIUM HEAT. ONCE IT BEGINS TO BOIL, REDUCE THE HEAT AND SIMMER UNTIL THE RICE IS COOKED THROUGH, FOR ABOUT 18-20 MINUTES.
9. PLACE THE COOKED DOLMADES ONTO A SERVING PLATTER, ADD SOME COOKING LIQUID OVER THE TOP, AND SERVE. THIS DISH CAN BE

ALSO SERVED AT ROOM TEMPERATURE.

Greek Vegan pasta

MOST OF US ARE FOND OF PASTA, BUT FEW OF US KNOW HOW TO COMBINE IT WITH BASIL, OREGANO AND GARLIC. WHILE TOMATOES ARE A USUAL DRESSING FOR PASTA, THE REST OF THE INGREDIENTS WILL SURPASS ALL YOUR EXPECTATIONS.

PREPARATION TIME 10 MINUTES
COOKING TIME 1 HR 20 MINUTES

SERVES: 4 - 6

INGREDIENTS:
1LB (454G) RIGATONI OR PENNE PASTA
2 TBSP BREAD CRUMBS
1 MEDIUM ONION, THINLY CHOPPED
2 GARLIC CLOVES, MINCED
1½ CUPS HOMEMADE OR CANNED TOMATO SAUCE, OR CRUSHED TOMATOES
1 CUP RED LENTILS
1½ CUPS VEGETABLE STOCK
1 TSP SALT
½ TSP BLACK PEPPER
1 TSP OREGANO
2 TBSP FRESH BASIL, CHOPPED
2 TBSP FRESH PARSLEY, CHOPPED

BÉCHAMEL
4OZ (113G) RAW CASHEWS
3 TBSP SUNFLOWER SEEDS
2 TBSP NUTRITIONAL YEAST
4 CUPS OF WATER
5 TBSP ALL PURPOSE FLOUR
5 TBSP OLIVE OIL OR VEGAN MARGARINE
1 TSP SALT
1 TSP NUTMEG, FRESHLY GRATED
1 TSP BLACK PEPPER, FRESHLY GROUND

DIRECTIONS:
1. ADD ¼ CUP OF WATER TO A MEDIUM SAUCEPAN AND SET OVER A MEDIUM HEAT. STIR IN THE GARLIC AND ONION, AND COOK UNTIL TENDER, FOR ABOUT 5 MINUTES.
2. ADD THE LENTILS, TOMATO SAUCE, VEGETABLE STOCK, OREGANO AND BASIL. SEASON WITH SALT AND PEPPER AND COOK FOR 20-22 MINUTES.
3. STIR IN THE PARSLEY AND CONTINUE COOKING FOR A FURTHER 3-4 MINUTES. ADD SOME WATER, IF NEEDED.
4. COOK THE PASTA IN A POT OF SALTED BOILING WATER UNTIL AL DENTE. DRAIN IN A COLANDER AND SET ASIDE. GENTLY COAT A BAKING DISH WITH OIL AND SPRINKLE WITH BREAD CRUMBS.
5. TRANSFER THE PASTA TO THE BAKING DISH AND TOP WITH THE LENTIL SAUCE.
6. PREHEAT THE OVEN TO 350°F (180°C).
7. TO MAKE THE BÉCHAMEL, PLACE THE SUNFLOWER SEEDS, CASHEW NUTS, YEAST, WATER, NUTMEG, SALT AND PEPPER INTO A BLENDER AND PULSE FOR 2-3 MINUTES.
8. TO MAKE THE ROUX, ADD THE FLOUR TO 5 TABLESPOONS OF HEATED OIL AND STIR-FRY OVER A MODERATE HEAT.
9. ADD THE CASHEW MIXTURE TO THE ROUX AND STIR FREQUENTLY. COOK THE MIXTURE FOR 5-6 MINUTES, UNTIL THE SAUCE HAS THICKENED.
10. TOP THE LENTIL MIXTURE WITH THE CASHEW BÉCHAMEL, AND SPRINKLE WITH BREADCRUMBS.
11. BAKE IN THE OVEN FOR 40 MINUTES, UNTIL GOLDEN BROWN AND FRAGRANT. SERVE HOT.

Braised Eggplant with Potatoes

THIS RECIPE INCLUDES THE CLASSIC GREEK TASTES: TOMATOES, ONIONS, POTATOES, EGGPLANT, HERBS AND OLIVE OIL. GIVE THIS A TRY AND ENJOY!

PREPARATION TIME 15 MINUTES
COOKING TIME 50 MINUTES
SERVES: 4

INGREDIENTS:
1LB (454G) EGGPLANT, CUT IN EGG-SIZED CHUNKS (NOT PEELED)
2LBS (907G) POTATOES, PEELED AND CUT
3 MEDIUM ONIONS, CHOPPED
1 BUNCH OF FRESH PARSLEY, CHOPPED
1½LBS (680G) FRESH TOMATOES, PULPED
OLIVE OIL
1½ CUPS OF WATER
1 TSP SALT
4 TBSP OF FLOUR

DIRECTIONS:
1. PLACE THE EGGPLANT PIECES IN A POT OF COLD WATER AND LET IT STAND FOR 30 MINUTES.
2. PLACE THE ONION, TOMATOES, ½ CUP OF OLIVE OIL, PARSLEY, 1¼ CUPS OF WATER AND ½ TEASPOON OF SALT INTO A MEDIUM SAUCEPAN, AND SET OVER A MEDIUM-HIGH HEAT.
3. ONCE BOILING, COVER AND REDUCE THE HEAT TO MEDIUM. COOK FOR 15 MINUTES. ADD THE POTATOES AND ¼ CUP OF WATER, COVER, AND CONTINUE COOKING UNTIL THE POTATOES ARE FORK TENDER, FOR ABOUT 15-20 MINUTES.
4. REMOVE THE EGGPLANT FROM THE WATER, DRAIN WELL, AND SPRINKLE WITH ½ TEASPOON OF SALT.
5. ADD 4 TABLESPOONS OF OLIVE OIL TO A

LARGE SKILLET AND PLACE OVER A HIGH HEAT.
6. COAT THE EGGPLANT PIECES WITH FLOUR AND SAUTÉ UNTIL GOLDEN BROWN ON BOTH SIDES.
7. TRANSFER THE EGGPLANT TO A PLATE LINED WITH PAPER TOWELS TO DRAIN.
8. ADD THE EGGPLANT TO THE SAUCEPAN OF VEGETABLE SAUCE AND SIMMER, COVERED, FOR A FURTHER 10 MINUTES. THIS DISH IS PERFECT SERVED EITHER HOT OR AT ROOM TEMPERATURE.

Quinoa Mushroom Pilaf

PILAF HAS HAD THOUSANDS OF FORMS AND HAS EXPERIENCED MILLIONS OF DRESSINGS, TRY THIS ONE TOO. GARLIC, PARSLEY, TOASTED NUTS, MUSHROOMS, BLACK PEPPER, AS WELL AS THE SOUR TASTE OF LEMON PROMISE AN INTERESTING EXPERIENCE.

READY IN 30 MINUTES
SERVES: 4 - 6

INGREDIENTS:
OLIVE OIL
2 CLOVES GARLIC, FINELY CHOPPED
1 MEDIUM YELLOW BELL PEPPER, FINELY DICED
1 MEDIUM GREEN BELL PEPPER, FINELY DICED
2 CUPS MUSHROOMS, SLICED
SEA SALT, TO TASTE
GROUND PEPPER, TO TASTE
2 TBSP FRESH PARSLEY, CHOPPED
1 TSP GREEK SEASONING (MINT, LEMON, BASIL, OREGANO MIX)
2 SCALLIONS (WHITE AND LIGHT GREEN SECTIONS), SLICED
SQUEEZE OF FRESH LEMON JUICE
EXTRA VIRGIN OLIVE OIL, TO TASTE
TOASTED PINE NUTS, FOR SERVING (OPTIONAL)

8. **DIRECTIONS:**
    1. THOROUGHLY WASH THE QUINOA AND DRAIN IN A FINE SIEVE. TRANSFER TO A RICE COOKER OR A LARGE SAUCEPAN, ADD TWO CUPS COLD WATER, COVER AND COOK UNTIL ALL THE LIQUID HAS BEEN EVAPORATED.
    2. MEANWHILE, ADD THE OIL TO A LARGE FRYING PAN AND SET OVER A MEDIUM HEAT.

3. ADD THE PEPPERS AND GARLIC TO THE PAN AND SAUTÉ, STIRRING FREQUENTLY, FOR 3-4 MINUTES, UNTIL JUST TENDER.
4. STIR IN THE MUSHROOMS AND SEASON WITH SEA SALT AND GROUND PEPPER. SPRINKLE WITH THE GREEK SEASONING AND STIR WELL TO COMBINE. COOK UNTIL THE MUSHROOMS HAVE SOFTENED.
5. STIR IN THE QUINOA, AND THEN ADD THE SLICED SCALLIONS.
6. DRIZZLE THE QUINOA WITH FRESH LEMON JUICE AND THE EXTRA VIRGIN OLIVE OIL. GENTLY STIR TO COMBINE. ADJUST SEASONINGS TO TASTE IF REQUIRED.
7. SPOON THE QUINOA PILAF ONTO A SERVING PLATE, GARNISH WITH TOASTED PINE NUTS AND CHOPPED PARSLEY IF DESIRE AND ENJOY.
8. THIS DISH CAN BE SERVED HOT, OR IT CAN BE CHILLED AND SERVED AS A SALAD.

Desserts

Fluffy Blueberry Waffles

MAKING THESE WAFFLES IS A REAL PARTY FOR THE WHOLE FAMILY. MAKE SURE THE KIDS ARE NOT AROUND, AS THEY WILL EAT ALL THE WAFFLES BEFORE YOUR GUESTS ARRIVE! TOP THEM WITH FRESH STRAWBERRIES, IF DESIRED, AND ENJOY.

PREPARATION TIME 15 MINUTES
COOKING TIME 10 MINUTES
SERVES: 4

INGREDIENTS:
2 CUPS WHOLE WHEAT ALL PURPOSE FLOUR
1 TBSP BAKING POWDER
¼ TSP SALT
⅓ CUP APPLE SAUCE
¼ CUP AGAVE NECTAR
1½ CUPS SOY MILK
1 TBSP OLIVE OIL
½ CUP BLUEBERRIES

9. **DIRECTIONS:**
1. COMBINE THE FLOUR, SALT AND BAKING POWDER IN A LARGE BOWL. IN A SEPARATE BOWL WHISK TOGETHER THE SOY MILK, APPLE

SAUCE, OLIVE OIL AND AGAVE NECTAR.
2. POUR THE MIXTURE OVER THE DRY INGREDIENTS AND MIX UNTIL INCORPORATED. LET THE BATTER STAND FOR 15 MINUTES.
3. ADD THE BLUEBERRIES AND STIR.
4. POUR THE BATTER INTO THE CENTER OF A WAFFLE IRON AND BAKE ACCORDING TO THE MANUFACTURER'S DIRECTIONS. REMOVE THE WAFFLES FROM THE WAFFLE MAKER USING A SPATULA.

BOBOTA

PREPARATION TIME 5 MINUTES
COOKING TIME 35 MINUTES
MAKES: 1 LOAF

INGREDIENTS:
2 CUPS CORNMEAL, OR COMBINATION OF CORNMEAL/CORN FLOUR
¾ CUP WATER AT ROOM TEMPERATURE
½ CUP FRESHLY SQUEEZED ORANGE JUICE
½ TSP CARDAMOMS, GROUND
1 TSP BAKING POWDER
½ TSP BAKING SODA
¼ TSP SALT
⅓ CUP SUGAR
3 TBSP OIL (SESAME, LIGHT OLIVE OR VEGETABLE)
2 TBSP ORANGE ZEST

10. **DIRECTIONS:**
1. PREHEAT THE OVEN TO 350°F (175°C).
2. IN A LARGE BOWL, SIEVE TOGETHER THE CORNMEAL, BAKING POWDER, SALT, BAKING SODA AND CARDAMOMS.
3. IN ANOTHER BOWL, DISSOLVE THE SUGAR IN THE WATER, STIRRING WITH A SPOON, THEN ADD THE ORANGE JUICE AND OIL, AND MIX WELL. POUR THE MIXTURE OVER THE DRY INGREDIENTS AND MIX UNTIL YOU HAVE A SMOOTH DOUGH.
4. ADD THE ORANGE ZEST, SLIGHTLY MIX, AND PLACE THE DOUGH INTO A BAKING LOAF PAN.
5. BAKE IN THE OVEN FOR ABOUT 35 MINUTES, UNTIL GOLDEN. INSERT A TOOTHPICK INTO THE CENTER TO CHECK WHEN THE LOAF IS COOKED. IF IT COMES OUT CLEAN THEN REMOVE FROM THE OVEN.

FINIKIA / MELOMACARONA

ONE-TWO STEPS AND THESE WONDERFUL SWEET AND CRUMBLY GREEK COOKIES ARE READY TO BE SERVED. THEY ARE GOOD IN ANY SHAPE AND FORM AND WILL CREATE A PLEASANT ATMOSPHERE ALONG WITH A CUP OF COFFEE OR TEA.

PREPARATION TIME 20 MINUTES
COOKING TIME 25 MINUTES
MAKES: 24 COOKIES

INGREDIENTS:

COOKIES
3½ CUPS OF ALL PURPOSE FLOUR
1 CUP OF VEGETABLE OIL
½ CUP ORANGE JUICE
⅓ CUP SUGAR
1 TSP ORANGE ZEST
½ TSP BAKING POWDER

¼ TSP BAKING SODA
½ TSP CINNAMON

SYRUP
½ CUP HONEY OR AGAVE NECTAR
1 CINNAMON STICK
¼ CUP SUGAR
1 – 1½ CUPS FRESHLY SQUEEZED ORANGE JUICE
½ CUP WATER
1 TBSP ORANGE ZEST

11. WALNUTS, PISTACHIOS, CHOPPED, TO GARNISH

12.

13. **INGREDIENTS**

1. MIX TOGETHER THE FLOUR, 1/3 CUP SUGAR, BAKING SODA, BAKING POWDER AND CINNAMON IN A LARGE BOWL AND SET ASIDE.

2. IN A MEDIUM BOWL, MIX TOGETHER THE SUGAR AND ORANGE JUICE, AND THEN WHISK IN THE VEGETABLE OIL. SET ASIDE.

3. IN ANOTHER LARGE BOWL, MIX TOGETHER THE WET AND DRY INGREDIENTS BY COMBINING ⅓ OF BOTH INGREDIENTS AT A TIME. YOU WILL FINISH WITH A SMOOTH DOUGH. LET THE DOUGH SIT FOR 15-20 MINUTES.

4. SHAPE SMALL BALLS FROM THE DOUGH AND THEN SLIGHTLY PAT THE BALLS TO FLATTEN. BAKE THE COOKIES IN A PREHEATED OVEN AT 350 F (175 C) FOR 25-28 MINUTES UNTIL THE EDGES ARE SLIGHTLY GOLDEN BROWN. LET THEM COOL.

5. MEANWHILE, IN A MEDIUM POT, MIX TOGETHER THE HONEY, SUGAR, ORANGE JUICE, ORANGE ZEST, CINNAMON STICK AND WATER, AND COOK OVER A LOW HEAT FOR ABOUT 10 MINUTES, STIRRING FREQUENTLY.

6. COAT THE COOKIES WITH THE WARM SYRUP ONCE COOKED. GARNISH WITH CHOPPED WALNUTS/PISTACHIOS AND SERVE.

WHEN YOU READ THE LIST OF INGREDIENTS FOR THIS CAKE YOU CAN APPRECIATE THAT YOU ARE ABOUT TO MAKE AN ABSOLUTELY DELICIOUS DESSERT, ONE THAT IS FULL OF VITAMINS AND PROTEINS. YOU CAN ALSO RELAX WITH THE KNOWLEDGE THAT THIS DISH WILL NOT HARM FOR YOUR DIET! TAKE TIME TO STORE THE CAKE IN THE REFRIGERATOR AND ENJOY IT ON THE NEXT DAY AS WELL.

PREPARATION TIME 40 MINUTES
COOKING TIME 1 HR 40 MINUTES 1HR 15 MINUTES
SERVES: 6

INGREDIENTS:
2 CUPS BAKED, MASHED APRICOTS (10-12 MEDIUM FRESH APRICOTS)
1 CUP ORANGE JUICE
3 CUPS ALL PURPOSE FLOUR
½ CUP ALMOND FLOUR/MEAL
1½ CUPS SUGAR
2 TSP BAKING POWDER
1 TSP BAKING SODA
¾ TSP SALT
½ CUP VEGETABLE OIL OR VERY LIGHT OLIVE OIL
2 TSP FRESHLY GROUND CARDAMOM (20 PODS)
1 TSP GROUND MAHLEP
1 CUP PISTACHIOS/ALMONDS OR WALNUTS, CHOPPED (OPTIONAL)

14. **DIRECTIONS:**
1. PREHEAT OVEN TO 400°F (200°C).
2. HALVE THE FRESH APRICOTS, REMOVING THE PIT. PLACE THEM ONTO A BAKING TRAY, SKIN SIDE DOWN, AND SLIGHTLY DRIZZLE WITH BRANDY OR WATER, IF DESIRED. TRANSFER THE APRICOTS INTO THE PREHEATED OVEN.
3. BAKE FOR 30-35 MINUTES. THEN REMOVE FROM THE OVEN AND COOL. GENTLY PEEL THE APRICOTS AND PUT THEM IN A MEDIUM SIZED BOWL. MASH AND SET ASIDE.
4. COMBINE THE ALMOND FLOUR, ALL PURPOSE FLOUR, BAKING SODA, BAKING POWDER, MAHLEP AND SALT IN A LARGE BOWL AND SET ASIDE.
5. IN A SMALL BOWL, WHISK TOGETHER THE SUGAR AND ORANGE JUICE, AND STIR IN THE CARDAMOM. GRADUALLY WHISK IN THE

VEGETABLE OIL AND MASHED APRICOTS.
6.   ADD THIS MIXTURE TO THE FLOUR MIXTURE AND WHISK TO COMBINE. STIR IN THE NUTS, IF USING.
7.   LINE A BAKING DISH WITH PARCHMENT. POUR THE BATTER INTO THE PREPARED DISH AND SPREAD EVENLY. IF BAKING IN A LOAF PAN, BAKE FOR 75 MINUTES; IF USING A 9×13INCH CAKE PAN, 45 MINUTES IS ENOUGH FOR THIS CAKE.
8.   ONCE THE TOP OF THE CAKE IS GOLDEN BROWN AND A KNIFE INSERTED IN THE CENTER COMES OUT CLEAN, REMOVE IT FROM THE OVEN AND COOL FOR 25-30 MINUTES IN THE BAKING PAN BEFORE SLICING.
9.   SLIGHTLY DUST THE COOKED CAKE WITH POWDERED SUGAR AND ENJOY.

TAHINI WALNUT TASTY COOKIES

PREPARATION TIME 15 MINUTES
COOKING TIME 25 MINUTES
MAKES: 18 COOKIES
INGREDIENTS:

COOKIES
3 CUPS FLOUR
1½ TSP BAKING POWDER
½ TSP SALT
½ CUP TOASTED ALMOND MEAL (FLOUR)
½ TSP CINNAMON
1 TSP GROUND MAHLEP
3 TBSP TAHINI
⅓ CUP SUGAR
1 CUP ORANGE JUICE
¼ CUP BRANDY

FILLING
1½ CUPS CHOPPED WALNUTS
⅓ CUP SUGAR
1 TSP CINNAMON
2 TBSP TAHINI
2 TBSP LEMON JUICE
2 TSP LEMON ZEST

15. **DIRECTIONS:**
1. PREHEAT OVEN TO 350ºF (175ºC).
2. IN A LARGE MIXING BOWL, MIX TOGETHER THE FLOUR, SALT, BAKING POWDER, ALMOND MEAL, CINNAMON AND MAHLEP, AND SET ASIDE.
3. IN A SEPARATE MEDIUM BOWL, MIX TOGETHER THE BRANDY AND ORANGE JUICE, THEN WHISK IN THE SUGAR AND TAHINI, AND SET ASIDE.
4. ADD THE BRANDY MIXTURE TO THE DRY INGREDIENTS AND MIX WELL TO FORM SMOOTH AND SOFT DOUGH. PLACE THE DOUGH IN THE

REFRIGERATOR, COVERED, UNTIL IT IS NEEDED.
5. TO START MAKING THE FILLING, PLACE THE SUGAR, CINNAMON, LEMON JUICE AND TAHINI IN A SMALL POT AND SET OVER A VERY LOW HEAT. KEEP STIRRING UNTIL THE MIXTURE RESEMBLES A THICK BROWN PASTE. ADD THE CHOPPED WALNUTS AND LEMON ZEST, AND MIX WELL TO COMBINE.
6. HALVE THE DOUGH INTO 2 BALLS. COAT THE WORKING SURFACE WITH FLOUR AND ROLL OUT 1 BALL INTO A THIN RECTANGLE.
7. EVENLY SPOON HALF OF THE WALNUT MIXTURE ON TOP OF THE RECTANGLE, SLIGHTLY PRESSING WITH A SPOON. GENTLY FOLD UP THE ROLLED DOUGH INTO A CYLINDER.
8. USING A SHARP KNIFE, CUT THE CYLINDER INTO THIN CIRCLES. REPEAT THIS WITH THE SECOND BALL OF DOUGH AND FILLING MIXTURE.
9. PLACE THE CIRCLES ONTO AN UN-GREASED BAKING DISH AND BAKE IN THE OVEN FOR 20-25 MINUTES. TRANSFER THE COOKIES TO A WIRE RACK TO COOL.
10. ENJOY.

Peach Barley

BAKED PEACHES MARRY THE BARLEY IN THE BEST POSSIBLE WAY IN THIS RECIPE, WHILE THE CINNAMON ADDS A LOVELY TANG TO THE WHOLE DISH.

PREPARATION 2 HRS
COOKING TIME 45 MINUTES
SERVES: 4 - 6

INGREDIENTS

1 CUP BARLEY
3 CUPS WATER
½ TSP SALT
3 TSP HONEY (OR AGAVE)
3 TBSP ORANGE JUICE
½ TSP CINNAMON
½ TSP GROUND CARDAMOM
2 WHOLE(2 CUPS CHOPPED) PEACHES (HALVED, ROASTED)
⅓ CUP FRESHLY CHOPPED MINT

16. **DIRECTIONS:**

1. PREHEAT THE OVEN TO 400°F (200°C). RINSE THE PEACHES UNDER COLD WATER, CUT IN HALF AND REMOVE THE PITS. PLACE THE PEACHES ONTO A BAKING TRAY, CUT SIDE UP.
2. IN A SMALL CUP, COMBINE EQUAL PARTS OF HONEY/AGAVE AND ORANGE JUICE, AND BRUSH THE MIXTURE OVER THE TOP OF THE PEACHES.
3. BAKE IN THE OVEN FOR ABOUT 25 MINUTES, UNTIL JUST SOFT. LET THEM COOL FOR A COUPLE OF MINUTES BEFORE GENTLY PEELING THE PEACHES AND CUTTING THEM INTO SMALL PIECES. SET ASIDE.
4. ADD BARLEY TO A POT OF SALTED WATER AND BRING TO A BOIL. REDUCE THE HEAT TO VERY LOW AND SIMMER 40-45 MINUTES, UNTIL TENDER.
5. IN A SMALL POT, MIX TOGETHER 3 TABLESPOONS ORANGE JUICE, 3 TABLESPOONS HONEY/AGAVE, CINNAMON AND CARDAMOM, AND PLACE OVER A VERY LOW HEAT FOR A FEW MINUTES UNTIL HEATED. SET ASIDE.
6. WHEN THE BARLEY IS DONE, PLACE IT IN A LARGE MIXING BOWL. POUR THE HOT HONEY MIXTURE OVER THE BARLEY AND STIR WELL TO COMBINE.
7. LET THE BARLEY MIXTURE COOL AND STIR IN THE CHOPPED MINT AND CHOPPED PEACHES.

8. PLACE THE BARLEY MIXTURE IN THE REFRIGERATOR AND REFRIGERATE FOR ABOUT 2 HOURS BEFORE SERVING.
9. PLACE THE CHILLED MIXTURE INTO SERVING BOWLS, SPRINKLE WITH RAISINS AND ANY TOASTED NUTS, GARNISH WITH FRESH PEACH SLICES AND ENJOY.

Greek Lenten Cake

THE SMELL ALONE OF THIS GREEK TAHINI CAKE, FLAVORED WITH CINNAMON, NUTMEG AND CLOVES IS WORTH THE TIME SPENT IN THE KITCHEN.

PREPARATION TIME 10 MINUTES
COOKING TIME 55 MINUTES
SERVES: 10 - 12

INGREDIENTS:
1 CUP TAHINI
¾ CUP SUGAR
1 ORANGE, GRATED
¾ CUP ORANGE JUICE
2¼ CUPS ALL PURPOSE FLOUR
1 DASH SALT
2½ TSP BAKING POWDER
½ TSP BAKING SODA
1 TSP CINNAMON
½ TSP NUTMEG
½ TSP CLOVE
½ TSP ALLSPICE
½ CUP WALNUTS (BROKEN INTO SMALL PIECES)
½ CUP SULTANA RAISINS

17. **DIRECTIONS:**
1. PREHEAT OVEN TO 350°F (180°C).
2. GENTLY COAT A LOAF PAN WITH OLIVE OIL AND THEN SLIGHTLY DUST WITH FLOUR.
3. IN A LARGE BOWL MIX TOGETHER THE

FLOUR, BAKING POWDER, BAKING SODA, CINNAMON, NUTMEG, CLOVE, ALLSPICE AND SEASON WITH SALT.

4.   IN A SEPARATE BOWL, USING A HAND-MIXER, WHIP THE TAHINI, ORANGE ZEST AND SUGAR UNTIL SMOOTH, FOR ABOUT 7-8 MINUTES.

5.   STIR IN THE ORANGE JUICE. GRADUALLY WHISK IN THE FLOUR MIXTURE. ONCE MIXED TOGETHER, ADD THE SULTANA RAISINS AND WALNUTS.

6.   ADD THE BATTER TO THE PREPARED BAKING PAN AND BAKE IN THE OVEN FOR 50-60 MINUTES, OR UNTIL A TOOTHPICK INSERTED IN THE CENTER COMES OUT CLEAN. LET IT COOL AND CUT INTO SQUARES BEFORE SERVING.

VEGAN CHOCOLATE NUT COOKIES

THIS IS REALLY A VERY INTERESTING DELICACY, WHICH MIGHT BECOME ONE OF YOUR FAVORITES FOR TREATING YOUR GUESTS.

PREPARATION TIME 10 MINUTES
COOKING TIME 5-10 MINUTES
MAKES: 36 COOKIES

INGREDIENTS:
⅓ CUP PEANUT BUTTER
2 TBSP CANOLA OIL
1 CUP SUGAR
⅓ CUP SOYMILK
1 TSP PURE VANILLA EXTRACT
1 CUP WHOLE WHEAT FLOUR
½ TSP BAKING SODA
½ TSP SALT
1 CUP FARINA
¼ CUP VEGAN CHOCOLATE CHIPS
¼ CUP CAROB CHIPS
½ CUP CHOPPED WALNUTS OR OTHER NUTS

18. **DIRECTIONS:**
    1. PREHEAT OVEN TO 425°F (220°C). COAT A BAKING DISH WITH OIL AND SET ASIDE.
    2. IN A LARGE MIXING BOWL, COMBINE THE SOYMILK, SUGAR, PEANUT BUTTER, CANOLA OIL AND VANILLA EXTRACT. MIX WELL UNTIL SMOOTH AND FLUFFY.
    3. GRADUALLY WHISK IN THE FLOUR, BAKING SODA, SALT, FARINA, CHOCOLATE AND CAROB CHIPS. FINALLY, FOLD IN THE CHOPPED NUTS/WALNUTS AND MIX WELL UNTIL BLENDED.
    4. USING A TEASPOON, DROP COOKIES 2 INCHES APART ON THE PREPARED BAKING SHEET, SLIGHTLY FLATTEN, AND BAKE FOR APPROXIMATELY 5 MINUTES, OR UNTIL THE TOP OF THE COOKIES ARE LIGHTLY BROWN.
    5. PLACE ON A WIRE RACK TO COOL.

GREEK HALVA

PREPARATION TIME 15 MINUTES
COOKING TIME 10 MINUTES
MAKES: 18 SERVINGS

INGREDIENTS:
1 CUP OLIVE OIL
2 CUPS GROUND SEMOLINA
2½ CUPS SUGAR (OR LESS)
1 TSP CINNAMON
4 CUPS HOT WATER
1 CUP RAISINS (OPTIONAL) OR 1 CUP NUTS (OPTIONAL)

DIRECTIONS:
1. ADD THE OLIVE OIL TO A HEAVY CAST SKILLET AND SET OVER A MEDIUM-HIGH HEAT. ADD THE SEMOLINA AND STIR-FRY FOR 3-4 MINUTES UNTIL LIGHTLY GOLDEN.
2. STIR IN THE SUGAR AND NUTS (IF USING), AND STIR-FRY FOR ANOTHER 3-4 MINUTES.
3. ONCE THE SEMOLINA BECOMES GOLDEN-BROWN, POUR IN THE HOT WATER.
4. REDUCE THE HEAT AND KEEP ON STIRRING UNTIL YOU HAVE A THICK MIXTURE. LET IT STAND FOR 10 MINUTES TO COOL.
5. PLACE THE HALVA INTO A RIMMED ROUND PAN, OR INTO INDIVIDUAL SERVING PLATES, SPRINKLE WITH CINNAMON AND NUTS/RAISINS AND ENJOY!

SPICY BAKED APPLES WITH HONEY SYRUP

WHEN YOU TRY THESE AMAZING APPLES YOU WILL FEEL LIKE YOU'RE IN HEAVEN! THE SERVING MUST ALSO BE AS DECENT AS THE DISH ITSELF TO PROVIDE THE BEST EXPERIENCE FOR THE GUESTS.
PREPARATION TIME 5 MINUTES
COOKING TIME 45 MINUTES
SERVINGS: 6

INGREDIENTS:
4 MEDIUM COOKING APPLES
¼ CUP WALNUTS, CHOPPED (OPTIONAL)
¼ CUP GOLDEN RAISINS
1 TSP HONEY
½ TSP GROUND CINNAMON
¼ TSP GROUND CLOVES
1 CUP WATER
1 CUP HONEY
1 TSP LEMON JUICE
1 CINNAMON STICK
WHIPPED CREAM (OPTIONAL)
DIRECTIONS:

1. PREHEAT THE OVEN TO 375°F (190°C). CAREFULLY CORE THE APPLES, MAKING SURE NOT TO CUT THROUGH THE BOTTOM.
2. IN A MEDIUM BOWL, MIX TOGETHER THE WALNUTS, RAISINS, GROUND CLOVES, CINNAMON AND HONEY.
3. USING A TEASPOON, POUR THIS MIXTURE INTO THE CENTER OF THE APPLES.
4. ARRANGE THE FILLED APPLES IN A BAKING PAN.
5. ADD THE HONEY, WATER, CINNAMON STICK AND LEMON JUICE TO A SMALL POT AND BRING THE MIXTURE TO A BOIL. COOK FOR 1-2 MINUTES, STIRRING CONSTANTLY.
6. DISREGARD THE CINNAMON STICK AND POUR THE HOT SYRUP OVER THE APPLES.
7. TRANSFER THE BAKING PAN TO THE OVEN AND BAKE FOR ABOUT 40 MINUTES. DURING THE BAKING BASTE THE APPLES 3-4 TIMES WITH THE PREPARED SYRUP.
8. ENJOY THE BAKED APPLES WARM OR COLD.
19.

CONCLUSION

WE HOPE YOU HAVE ENJOYED USING THIS COOKBOOK WHICH IS FULL OF CHEF D'OEUVRES OF GREEK COOKING. THE GREEK CUISINE IS REAL HEAVEN FOR GOURMANDS.

I AM SURE YOU HAVE NOTICED THAT THE BASIS OF THE RECIPES IS HEALTHY FOOD, INCLUDING FRESH VEGETABLES, FRUITS, GRAINS, OLIVE OIL, BEANS AND MANY OTHER INGREDIENTS WHICH WILL PROVIDE YOU WITH A VALUABLE ENERGY SUPPLY THAT YOUR BODY NEEDS.

EVERY RECIPE HAS BEEN DEVELOPED WITH THE INTENTION TO MAKE YOUR TIME IN THE KITCHEN

EASY AND ENJOYABLE. WE HAVE PRESENTED TO YOU SOME OF THE EASIEST, YET HEALTHIEST PREPARATION METHODS WHICH YOU CAN APPLY TO MAKE YOUR FOOD BOTH FULFILLING AND DELICIOUS.

HOPEFULLY THIS COOKBOOK WAS ABLE TO HELP YOU TO VERIFY YOUR MENU IN PREPARING A HEALTHY AND DELICIOUS GREEK MEAL.

www.ingramcontent.com/pod-product-compliance
Lightning Source LLC
LaVergne TN
LVHW020427070526
838199LV00004B/305